ANSWERS TO QUESTIONS

PHYSICS

PRINCIPLES WITH APPLICATIONS

Fifth Edition

ANSWERS TO QUESTIONS

GORDON AUBRECHT
Ohio State University

MICHELE RALLIS
Ohio State University

KURT REIBEL
Ohio State University

PHYSICS

PRINCIPLES WITH APPLICATIONS

Fifth Edition

GIANCOLI

PRENTICE HALL, Upper Saddle River, NJ 07458

Executive Editor: *Alison Reeves*
Production Editor: *Carole Suraci*
Special Projects Manager: *Barbara A. Murray*
Supplement Cover Manager: *Paul Gourhan*
Production Coordinator: *Ben Smith*

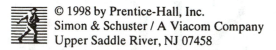 © 1998 by Prentice-Hall, Inc.
Simon & Schuster / A Viacom Company
Upper Saddle River, NJ 07458

Printed in the United States of America

10 9 8 7 6 5 4 3 2 1

ISBN 0-13-095099-8

Prentice-Hall International (UK) Limited, *London*
Prentice-Hall of Australia Pty. Limited, *Sydney*
Prentice-Hall Canada, Inc., *Toronto*
Prentice-Hall Hispanoamericana, S.A., *Mexico*
Prentice-Hall of India Private Limited, *New Delhi*
Prentice-Hall of Japan, Inc., *Tokyo*
Simon & Schuster Asia Pte. Ltd., *Singapore*
Editora Prentice-Hall do Brasil, Ltda., *Rio de Janeiro*

Table of Contents

Chapter 1

1.   Standards need to be accessible, indestructible, invariable, and reproducible so that people can be sure they are measuring what they think they are measuring. Our present standards of time and length, defined in terms of the frequency of a certain type of radiation emitted by a cesium atom and the speed of light in vacuum, respectively, are universal and indestructible, but accessibility to these "natural" standards is limited to laboratories equipped to deal with them.

Secondary standards, such as those at various national standards laboratories, can be calibrated against these natural standards, and then used to provide tertiary standards to industry. These secondary and tertiary standards are much more accessible and, if recalibrated at regular intervals, adequately accurate.

2.   a) A particular person's foot is not very accessible, although secondary standards could be made, as long as everybody agreed on that particular person's foot. The standard is not indestructible and, depending on the precision required, not invariable (feet swell up, etc.).

Any person's foot is very accessible but not invariable at all, as any shoe salesman will verify. Such a length standard could easily vary by a factor of two and thus, would be unsatisfactory.

3.   Put the signs at 1000 m (3,281 ft), etc. Then the feet will seem more complicated. Look at speedometers on recent U.S. cars. You will find two sets of tick marks and labels, one in miles per hour, the other in kilometers per hour, both independently calibrated at easily read intervals. However, in the early days, some of the speedometers had a single set of tick marks labeled 10, 20, 30, ... mph with the corresponding values of 15, 32, 48, ... km/h attached to the same tick marks. This made the metric system seem more complicated.

4.   a) Giancoli was probably thinking of triangulation, using the radius of Earth as known. For example, simultaneously measure the Sun's location in the reference frame of the background stars from positions A and B on Earth, separated by 90°. Using the radius of Earth (R) as known and measuring the small angle (about 9") allows you to solve the right triangle for the distance of the Sun. There are technical problems in doing this: the Sun does not have a sharp edge and since background stars are not visible in daytime, you need a telescope whose orientation in the reference frame of the background stars can be set automatically with an accuracy better than 1". This could be achieved using a telescope orbiting Earth above the atmosphere.

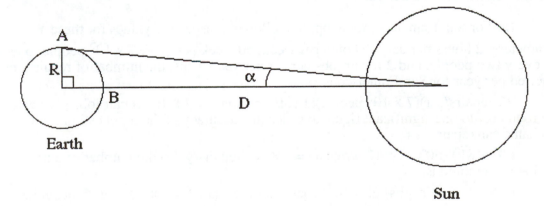

4., continued

Alternatively, one may use the angle in the sky between the Sun and the Moon when the Moon is in first quarter phase and the distance from Earth to the Moon. The orientation of the Sun, Moon, and Earth at this phase is shown in the diagram below. The first quarter Moon is visible in the daytime; it rises at noon. If you measure the angular separation θ (about 89° 51') on the sky and use the Earth-Moon distance as known, you can solve the right triangle for the distance of the Sun.

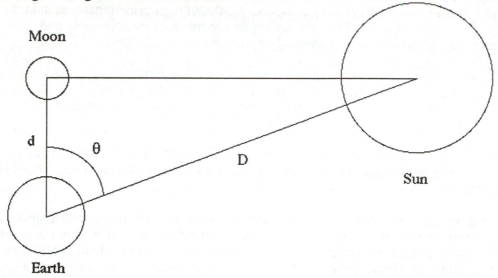

In practice, the distance of the Sun is determined indirectly by measuring the distance of Earth to another planet and using this to calibrate the scale of the solar system.

5.   The sign gives the distance in miles to one significant figure, but it gives the distance in kilometers to five significant figures. The distance should be specified to the same number of significant figures in each unit.

6.   To estimate the number of auto mechanics, we estimate average values for the following: the number of hours it takes an auto mechanic to repair one car, the number of hours the auto mechanic works per week, the number of weeks the auto mechanic works per year, the population of the city, the number of cars per person, and the number of times that each car is repaired per year.

(a) For San Francisco, we adopt the following respective values for these parameters: 2 hours per car, 40 hours per week, 50 week per year, 7×10^5 people, one car for every two people, and 2 repair jobs per car per year. Thus, the number of repair jobs required per year for San Francisco is

(2 repairs/car)(7×10^5 people)(1 car/2 persons) = 7×10^5 repair jobs per year. We round off to one significant figure to reflect the accuracy of the input estimates. One mechanic can repair

(40 h/wk) (50 wk/y)/(2 h/repair) = 1×10^3 repairs/y. So the number of auto mechanics required is

(7×10^5 repair jobs)/(1×10^3 repairs per mechanic) = 7×10^2 auto mechanics.

6., continued

(b) We now scale this number to make an estimate for Columbus, Ohio. The population of Columbus is 6×10^5. There are probably more cars per person in Columbus because San Francisco has a better public transportation system. For Columbus, we take 2 cars for every 3 people, so we multiply 7×10^2 auto mechanics by

$(6 \times 10^5$ people$/7 \times 10^5$ people$)$ $(0.7$ cars per person$/0.5$ cars per person$)$.

This gives 8×10^2 for the estimated number of auto mechanics in Columbus.

In the Columbus, Ohio metropolitan area, there are 15 columns of auto repair shops in the telephone book. Counting the number of repair shops per column in two columns gives an average of 25 shops per column. If each repair shop employs 3 auto mechanics on the average, then the estimated number of auto mechanics in the Columbus metropolitan area is

$(3$ mechanics per shop$)(25$ shops/column$)(15$ columns$) = 1 \times 10^3$,

where we round off to 1 significant figure since the number of mechanics per shop is estimated to only one significant figure. The metropolitan area has a population of over 1×10^6, so for the city of Columbus, this would give an estimate of 6×10^2 auto mechanics, which is consistent with our first estimate.

7.   For grades 1 through 12, the average number of hours spent in school per school day = 6.0 and the average number of school days per year = 180 (this is the minimum number of school days per year mandated by law in certain states). Thus, for grades 1 through 12, the estimated number of hours spent in school is

$(6.0$ h/d$)\times(180$ d/yr$)\times(12$ yr$) = 1.3 \times 10^4$ h.

This is given to two significant figures since that is the minimum number of significant figures in the data.

Add to this the time spent in class in college. Assume that in college the average number of hours spent in class per week is 15 and that the average length of the school year is 33 weeks. So if you are starting your junior year in college, you will have spent an estimated time in college in class of

$(15$ h/wk$)\times(33$ wk/yr$)\times(2.0$ yr$) = 9.9 \times 10^2$ h.

Adding this to the time spent in school in grades 1 through 12 gives a total estimated time of 1.4×10^4 h, where again the answer is given to two significant figures.

8.   Assume that each marble has the same radius R. To estimate the space required per marble, assume that the marbles form a rectangular lattice in which each marble touches 6 other marbles, i.e., one on the left, one on the right, one on the top, one on the bottom, one in front, and one behind. Although the marbles at the edges of the jar don't touch 6 other marbles, they require about the same amount of space as the marbles in the interior. The estimated space required for each marble is a cube of side 2R and, therefore, volume $(2R)^3$. If V is the volume of the jar, then the estimated number of marbles in the jar is $V/(8R^3)$. (The configuration is more likely to be close-packed hexagonal, which would reduce the volume per marble.)

9.   In the equation, diameter = 2 times the radius, the factor of 2 is a pure number, not a measured value, so it has no uncertainty. Therefore, the correct answer is 8.32 cm.

Chapter 2

1. A car's speedometer measures speed only.

2. An object can have a varying velocity if its speed is constant. Since velocity is a vector, it has both magnitude and direction. The magnitude is called speed and any motion with constant speed but changing *direction* will have a varying velocity. Circular motion at constant speed is an example.

3. If an object has varying speed, its velocity is not constant, since the magnitude of the velocity vector is changing.

4. No. If velocity is constant, its average velocity always equals its instantaneous velocity, because in that case the velocity during any time interval has the same constant value, even as $\Delta t \to 0$.

5. The car with the greatest speed crossing the finish line is not necessarily the first car to cross the finish line since its speed could have varied during the race. The car with the highest speed at the finish line could have traveled most of the race more slowly than the other cars and accelerated to high speeds only just before it reached the finish line. Or, during the race, it could have stopped to change a flat tire as all the other cars passed, and then, even though it had the highest speed in the latter part of the race, it could not catch up. If the race is in a straight line so that each car travels the same distance, then the car with the highest *average* speed will arrive at the finish line first.

6. No; for example, both objects may have zero acceleration now. Suppose cars A and B are accelerated from rest with the same acceleration, but car A is accelerated for a longer time interval. Then car A will end up with the greater speed. Or consider two falling objects. If air resistance is neglected, both have the same downward acceleration, but when viewed at the same instant, the object dropped first has the greater speed.

7. We treat this as a one-dimensional problem, so only speed is involved. In both cases the change in speed during the same time interval is the same, i.e.,

$$a_{av} = \frac{(90\text{-}80)\text{ km/h}}{\Delta t} = \frac{(10\text{-}0)\text{ km/h}}{\Delta t},$$

and the acceleration is same.

8. The speedometer indicates only the instantaneous speed (in miles per hour and, in recent U.S. cars, in km/h also). If the instantaneous speed on the speedometer is changing, then you are accelerating, but the speedometer does not give you a numerical value for the acceleration. Also, the readings on the speedometer would not let you know that you are accelerating when you drive around a curve at a constant speed.

9. Acceleration is defined as the *change* in velocity with time and does not depend on the value of the velocity itself. Therefore, an object can have a northward velocity and a southward acceleration. Example: you are driving due north and hit the brakes.

10. Yes and Yes. Take northward to be negative in Question 9 above for an illustration of the first case. For an example of the second case drive southward and hit the brakes.

11.　　If we take downward as negative and throw a stone upward, velocity will initially be positive, go to zero at the highest point, and become negative when falling down, while the acceleration is always negative. Thus, while the stone is falling, both its velocity and acceleration are negative.

12.　　Yes. Drop a ball and choose downward as negative. Since the acceleration is down, it is negative, but the speed of the ball will increase as it falls.

13.　　Since the cars emerge side by side and Car A is traveling faster than Car B, Car A is passing Car B at that instant.

Indeed, provided the accelerations of the cars do not change, it takes one minute for both cars to reach the same speed; this is obtained by equating $(v_0 + at)$ for Car A to $(v_0 + at)$ for Car B. During the one minute interval, the displacement from the tunnel,

$$x - x_0 = v_0 t + \frac{1}{2} at^2,$$

is 1.33 km for Car A and 1.17 km for Car B, so Car A is many car lengths ahead of Car B.

14.　　Yes, the speed of the object can increase while the magnitude of its acceleration is decreasing if the velocity and the acceleration are both in the same direction. The acceleration describes the rate of change of the velocity and if both are in the same direction, the speed of the object will increase.

Suppose at time t_1 you are driving due north with your foot depressing the gas pedal so that the speed of the car is increasing rapidly (large acceleration). Then an instant later, at time t_2, you let up on the gas pedal slightly, so that the speed of the car is still increasing but not as rapidly as before (smaller acceleration). At both instants the velocity and the acceleration are in the same direction, so the velocity increases, but the magnitude of the acceleration has decreased from time t_1 to time t_2.

15.　　Its acceleration due to gravity is independent of the motion of the freely falling object, so it remains the same.

16.　　To estimate how fast you can throw the ball, throw the ball vertically upwards and measure the time t to reach maximum altitude. Neglecting air resistance and choosing up to be the positive direction, the acceleration of the ball = -g, and since its velocity at maximum altitude = 0, its initial velocity

$$v_0 = v - at = gt = (9.8 \text{ m/s}^2)t.$$

Its maximum altitude is

$$y - y_0 = v_0 t + \frac{1}{2} at^2 = gt^2 - \frac{1}{2} gt^2 = \frac{1}{2} gt^2.$$

Note that all you have to measure is the time t (or measure the time for the round trip and divide by 2).

17.　　If air resistance is taken into account, speed is lost both going up (maximum height attained will be less) and coming down, with the result that, when the object returns to its original position, its speed will be less than the initial speed with which it was thrown up.

18.   Consider one-dimensional motion along x. It starts at $x = 0$ at constant speed for about 20 s, increases speed and then slows down to zero at around 37 s, where displacement is 20 m; then it reverses direction, speeds up, slows down and comes to rest after 50 s at $x = 10$ m.

19.   Consider one-dimensional motion. An object with initial speed of 14 m/s undergoes constant positive acceleration of 0.5 m/s^2 for about 45 s during which time (using $x = v_0 t + \frac{1}{2} a t^2$) it moves about 1200 m and its speed increases to 38 m/s. The acceleration goes to zero when that speed is reached and reverses sign and goes to zero again at 90 s, when v has also dropped to zero.

During the negative acceleration period, the object moves about another 700 m. The object remains at rest from 90 s to 108 s, and then undergoes positive acceleration from 108 s to 125 s, when its speed reaches 12 m/s. This gains another 100 m displacement for the object, for a total displacement of 2000 m during the 125 s, giving an average speed of 16 m/s.

Chapter 3

1.   Both odometer and speedometer measure scalar quantities. The odometer measures distance, the speedometer the instantaneous speed. Neither is concerned with direction.

2.   The vectors must have the same magnitude but opposite directions.

3.   The displacement vector can never be longer than the path length, since it is the straight line distance between the beginning and end points and thus, the shortest distance between them. It will generally be less than the path length unless the path is unidirectional along the displacement vector, in which case the length of the displacement vector will equal the path length.

4.   They both had the same displacement. Displacement is defined as the vector between initial and final positions, and both player and ball have identical ones.

5.   No. It depends on the magnitude and direction of the two vectors. If both are of the same magnitude and opposite in direction, then $V = 0$. If $V_1 = 10$ and $V_2 = 1$ and they are in opposite directions, then $V = 9$, which is less than V_1 but greater than V_2.

6.   Max = 4.0 km + 3.5 km = 7.5 km (in same direction); Min = 4.0 km - 3.5 km = 0.5 km (in opposite directions).

7.   a) No. Unless they are of equal magnitude, two vectors cannot have a resultant of zero.
        b) Yes. Three unequal vectors can have a resultant of zero if they can form the sides of a triangle.

8.   a) Yes, if the other components are zero.
        b) No, since the magnitude equals the square root of the sum of the squares of the components.

9.   No, because $|V| = (V_x{}^2 + V_y{}^2 + V_z{}^2)^{1/2} = 0$ implies $V_x = V_y = V_z = 0$.

10.   The velocities of a car traveling due east at 50 km/h and one traveling north at 50 km/h are NOT equal, since their directions differ. For vectors to be equal, they must have the same magnitude and the same direction.

11.   A projectile has the least speed at the highest point in its path, where the vertical component is zero.

12.   In both cases, one wants maximum launch speed v_0 , but for the high jump the departure angle should be greater than for the long jump.
        A) Long jump: if air resistance is neglected, the value of θ that gives the greatest range x is 45° (see example 3.7).

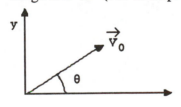

B) High jump : The altitude reached is given by $2gy = (v_{y0})^2 = (v_0 \sin \theta)^2$. Thus, jumping in place ($\theta = 90°$) would produce the highest jump for a given value of v_0. However, in doing the high jump, one must jump over the bar so $\vec{v}_0$ must have a horizontal component. Thus, one wants θ to be large but less than 90°.

13.   Using only a meter stick determine the speed of a rock by firing a slingshot horizontally and measuring height of the slingshot above ground and the range of rock. Here, $v_0 = v_x$; $h = \frac{1}{2} gt^2$; $t = (2h/g)^{1/2}$; and $x = v_x t$. Therefore, $v_x = \dfrac{x}{t} = \dfrac{x}{(2h/g)^{1/2}}$.

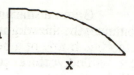

14.   You adopt your moving train, not the ground, as the reference frame for measuring velocity. In the reference frame of the faster train, the slower train is moving backwards: the velocity of the slower train relative to the faster train $= v_{slow} - v_{fast}$.

15.

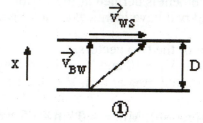 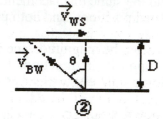

In both cases, $t = \dfrac{D}{v_x}$. The velocity $\vec{v}_{BW}$ is the velocity of the boat relative to the water.

① $v_x = v_{BW}$.

② $v_x = v_{BW} \cos \theta < v_{BW}$, so $t_1 < t_2$.

Chapter 4

1.   Given a sharp pull, the wagon and the lower body parts of the child in frictional contact with the wagon will accelerate, while the unsupported upper body will not. In the reference frame of a person at rest with respect to the ground, the upper body remains at rest, while the lower parts are accelerated forward. In the frame of the cart, the upper body falls backward.

2.   An apple has a mass in the range 0.1 to 0.3 kg and, therefore, weighs 1 to 3 newtons.

3.   If the acceleration of a body is zero, the net force on it is zero. This could be due either to forces acting on it that cancel out, or no forces acting on it.

4.   You have to pedal a bicycle harder when first starting out than while moving at constant speed, because you are accelerating. After reaching constant speed (assuming a horizontal road) you pedal only to overcome friction and air resistance.

5.   If only one force acts on an object, it is the net force, and according to the Second Law there must be acceleration. If the initial velocity is in a direction opposite to the force, the object will slow down, reach zero velocity, and then accelerate in the direction of the force. This is what happens when you throw a ball straight up. Thus, it can have zero velocity instantaneously.

6.   a)Yes.
                        b)The pavement. The ball exerts a force down on the pavement and, by Newton's Third Law, the pavement exerts a normal force upwards on the ball.

7.   The external force exerted by the ground on you is necessary to accelerate you forward (Newton's Second Law), while the forces that you exert on your legs are involved in changing which foot is in front. Starting with both feet on the ground, one forward of the other, there are no horizontal forces, and the vertical forces cancel, and you are momentarily at rest (Newton's First Law). While raising the heel of your rear foot (Newton's Second Law), you lean forward so that your weight will be over your front foot. To transfer your weight forward, you must exert a contact force backwards on the ground with your feet, and the ground exerts an equal and opposite force (Newton's Third Law) to accelerate you forward (Newton's Second Law). You raise your rear foot off the ground (Newton's Second Law) and continue to push backwards on the ground with your other foot so that the reaction force of the ground will accelerate you forward (Newton's Second Law). Thus, when your raised foot returns to the ground as a result of the force of gravity (Newton's Second Law), it will be ahead of the other foot. The forces now balance and you are momentarily at rest again (Newton's First Law).

8.   These objects do not move significantly because of their large masses. Therefore, you can exert a very large force on them, and, by the Third Law, they will exert an equally large force your foot. If you kick a ball, the force you can exert on it, and consequently, the force the ball exerts on your foot, is limited by the fact that the ball, having small mass, moves quickly away.

9.   a) Friction with the ground. The soles of your feet will be pushing forward on the ground and by the Third Law, the ground will exert a backward force on you.
      b) Assume speed of 3 m/s and stopping distance of 5 m. Then,

$$a = \frac{v^2}{2x} = \frac{9}{10} \text{ m/s}^2, \text{ or about } \frac{1}{10} \text{ g.}$$

10.   The thread breaks in the region of maximum tension. Call the section of the thread dangling below the stone the *bottom* thread, and the section of the thread above the stone, the *top* thread. The picture shows the forces exerted on the stone.

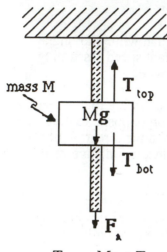

mass M

T_{top}

Mg

T_{bot}

F_a

a) A sharp pull on the bottom thread accelerates the bottom thread. The force F_a is applied to the bottom thread, which then applies a force T_{bot} to the stone. The bottom thread has a greater downward acceleration than the stone because the stone has greater inertia. The lower part of the bottom thread accelerates down before the stone and the top thread. This means that with a sufficiently large acceleration, the bottom thread will break. Because of the large mass, T_{bot} can exert a large force on M, whose Newton's Third Law ("reaction") force is equally great; this results in a large tension that can break the bottom string.

b) Treat a slow, steady pull as if the acceleration is approximately zero. In this approximation, the net force on the stone is zero, so

$$T_{top} = Mg + T_{bot}$$

Thus, $T_{top} > T_{bot}$ and the top thread breaks.

11.   From Newton's Second Law, a = F/m, where F is the net force, in this case, the force of gravity. Thus, if one doubles the mass of the rock and doubles the net force on the rock, the acceleration will be the same. All objects have the same gravitational acceleration, independent of mass.

12.   a) Since gravitational acceleration on the Moon is about one-sixth that on Earth, the force needed to lift a 10 kg object on the Moon will be one-sixth that on Earth, i.e., 16 N instead of 98 N.

      b) The force needed to throw a 2 kg object horizontally with a given speed will be the same on the Moon as on Earth since the gravitational acceleration does not enter into this case.

13.   The rear end collision suddenly accelerates the car forward. The seat in which the person is sitting is accelerated along with the car and so is that portion of the person's body supported by the seat. If the head is not supported, it will not accelerate along with the body, and with reference to the frame of the car and the body, it will appear to have been thrown backward. For an observer in the street the head remains at rest and the car, seat, and body are jerked forward. Regardless of reference frame the whiplash injury will be real.

14.   If person exerts an upward force $F_{P \text{ on } M}$ of 40 N on a bag of groceries of mass M, then by Newton's Third Law the "reaction" force $F_{M \text{ on } P}$

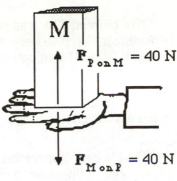

a) has magnitude of 40 N.
b) is directed downward.
c), d) is exerted *by* the bag *on* the person.

15.   The ground exerts a force equal to your weight so that the net vertical force on you is zero and you don't accelerate vertically.

16.   The winning team in a tug-of-war is the one that can dig its heels in the ground better. Consider both teams and the rope as a single system. If this system is to accelerate, a net external force must be exerted on it. This force is exerted by the ground in reaction to the force exerted on the ground by the participants' feet. The team that exerts the greater force on the ground wins.

17.   Unless you apply the brakes slowly (either by "pumping" or by letting an Antilock Braking System do it for you) the wheels will stop turning (lock up) and your car will start sliding ("skidding") and you would lose control of your car.

18.   The train has much more mass and it would take a correspondingly greater force to stop it in the same distance. Unfortunately, there is no way a train can exert such a braking force. Even with all wheels locked, it would slide a significant distance along the tracks before coming to rest.

19.   Yes. Try sliding velcro surfaces over each other!

20.   On the ascent, both the component of the gravitational force parallel to the ramp and the frictional force point down the ramp, while on the descent the frictional force points up the ramp and thus, opposes the gravitational force, leading to a smaller net downward force and, by the Second Law, a smaller magnitude of acceleration.

21.   The frictional force between the crate and the bed of the truck.

22.   The force of friction is parallel to the surface, and in this case, acts vertically upward to keep the box from slipping down. In magnitude, the maximum force of static friction equals the coefficient of static friction times the normal force. When you push harder horizontally on the box, the normal force exerted on the box by the wall will increase to keep the net force on the box zero in the horizontal direction. (Note that the normal force exerted on the box by the wall is in the horizontal direction.) The increase in the normal force causes the magnitude of the maximum friction force to increase and this keeps the box from slipping.

Chapter 5

1.   Not correct. The water is removed from the clothes because there is insufficient centripetal force on it to keep it rotating with the clothes during the spin cycle and, therefore, it flies off tangentially.

2.   Acceleration of car at 60 km/h around a sharp curve will be greater than that around a gentle curve at same speed, since $a = \dfrac{v^2}{r}$ and r is less for sharp curve than for gentle one.

3.   Here we are concerned only with vertical forces. The force the car exerts on the road is equal and opposite to the force the road exerts on the car (Newton's Third Law).
       a) At the top of a hill, the net force on the car is the downward centripetal force F_c, which equals the downward weight of the car minus the upward normal force of the road on the car; thus, $F_c = W - N$, or $N = W - F_c$ (least force).
       b) At the dip, the centripetal force is upward and $N = W + F_c$ (greatest force).
       c) On the level stretch, $F_c = 0$ and $N = W$.

4.   The forces on the child are her weight acting down, the normal force exerted by the (solid) horse acting upward, the radially inward force the horse exerts to keep her going in a circle, the reaction forces to whatever forces her hands exert on the merry-go-round's pole, etc. The child's centripetal acceleration is provided by the contact force the horse exerts on her in the radially inward direction.

5.   If the speed of the bucket at the top is such that the centripetal force on the water is equal to or greater than the weight of the water, it will not spill out. The weight of the water (plus any additional necessary downward force exerted by the bucket on the water) provides the centripetal force necessary to make the water go in a circle.

6.   The force the apple exerts on Earth is equal in magnitude to the force Earth exerts on the apple, namely the weight of the apple, $F_{\text{Earth-apple}} = G \dfrac{M_{\text{apple}} M_{\text{Earth}}}{r_{\text{Earth}}^2} = W_{\text{apple}} = M_{\text{apple}}\, g$ (we assume the apple's at the surface of Earth). This is the same whether the apple is attached to a tree or is falling.

7.   Setting the gravitational force on the Moon equal to its mass times its centripetal acceleration gives the following relation between the Moon's orbital period T, the radius R of the Moon's orbit around Earth, and the mass M_E of Earth (see Section 5-8):
$$\frac{T^2}{R^3} = \frac{4\pi^2}{GM_E}.$$
The orbital speed $v = 2\pi R/T$.

If Earth's mass were double its present value, then $M'_E = 2M_E$ and, hence,
$$\frac{T'^2}{R'^3} = \frac{1}{2}\frac{T^2}{R^3}.$$

This is one equation with two unknowns and has no unique solution for T' and R'. For example:

       a) If we keep the Moon at its present distance, then its new period T' decreases to $T/\sqrt{2}$ and its new orbital speed v' increases to $\sqrt{2}\, v$.

Chapter 5

7., continued

b) If we keep the period the same as present, then its new radius $R' = 2^{1/3} R$ and its new orbital speed $v' = 2^{1/3} v$.

c) If we keep the orbital speed the same as at present, then $\dfrac{T'}{T} = \dfrac{R'}{R}$, so $R' = 2R$ and $T' = 2T$.

8. Since metal ores are denser than the surrounding soil or rock, they will cause local increases in the value of g. By carefully mapping these variations, the locations and amounts of ore can be determined.

9. Apparent weight is greatest in b), less in a), zero in c), and the same as on the ground in d).

10. The tangential velocity and the centripetal acceleration a_c of material composing Earth's surface are largest at the Equator. Material at latitude θ is spinning in a circle of radius $r = R \cos θ$, where R is Earth's radius. It has tangential speed $v = 2πr/T$, where T is the rotation period of Earth, so the speed v is greatest at the Equator and
$$a_c = v^2/r = 4 π^2 r/T^2 = 4 π^2 R \cos θ/T^2$$
is greatest at the Equator (θ = 0), where it equals 3.4×10^{-2} m/s^2.

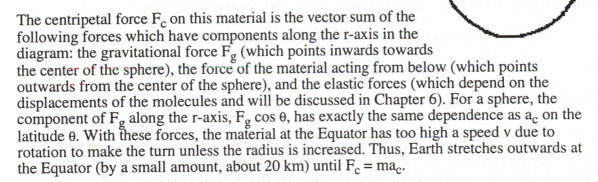

The centripetal force F_c on this material is the vector sum of the following forces which have components along the r-axis in the diagram: the gravitational force F_g (which points inwards towards the center of the sphere), the force of the material acting from below (which points outwards from the center of the sphere), and the elastic forces (which depend on the displacements of the molecules and will be discussed in Chapter 6). For a sphere, the component of F_g along the r-axis, $F_g \cos θ$, has exactly the same dependence as a_c on the latitude θ. With these forces, the material at the Equator has too high a speed v due to rotation to make the turn unless the radius is increased. Thus, Earth stretches outwards at the Equator (by a small amount, about 20 km) until $F_c = ma_c$.

11. The antenna will continue to orbit Earth alongside the satellite since it has the same speed and centripetal acceleration. The only way to bring it back to Earth would be to reduce its orbital speed sufficiently to cause it to spiral down. In a low Earth orbit ,there is enough residual atmospheric friction to cause this to happen within a few decades.

At the altitude of a geosynchronous satellite, the antenna would remain aloft for a very, very long time unless it were hit by a meteor or another piece of space junk. (There is some friction even in interplanetary space since interplanetary space is not a perfect vacuum.)

12. Note that rotating reference frames are treated in Appendix C, not Ch. 5. The people inside a rotating shell find themselves in a non-inertial reference frame and experience pseudoforces. In particular, they feel a centrifugal force, which acts radially outward and simulates gravity. This gravity is strongest at the periphery and vanishes at the spin axis.

12., continued

      a) Objects will fall radially outward.

      b) The force on the feet is upward, just as it is in real gravity. (Seen from an inertial frame, this is, of course, the centripetal force that keeps the person rotating in uniform circular motion).

      c) They can put objects down and they will stay put. They can drink liquids without messing up, etc.

13.   The gravitational force of Earth on the Moon has the same magnitude as the gravitational force of the Moon on Earth. This follows from Newton's Third Law; it can also be seen directly in Newton's Law of Universal Gravitation. Since the Moon has the smaller mass, it has the larger acceleration. In both cases, the acceleration is directed radially inward (that is, it is a centripetal acceleration).

14.   The controls in the car that can cause the car to accelerate are the gas pedal, the steering wheel, the brake pedal, the shift, the parking brake, and the ignition key.

Depressing the gas pedal can cause the car to increase speed, whereas letting up on the gas pedal can cause the car to decrease speed as a result of friction between the tires and the road. An increase in speed or a decrease in speed are both accelerations.

Turning the steering wheel changes the direction of the velocity; this is at least partly a centripetal acceleration.

When the car is in motion, depressing the brake pedal, setting the parking brake, downshifting, or turning off the ignition (this should be done only in an emergency situation in which the other controls fail) causes the car to decrease speed, which is an acceleration. If parked on a steep hill, releasing the parking brake can result in the car starting to roll down the hill.

15.   To explain the decrease in the normal force F_N on the child, use the following two free-body diagrams and Newton's Second Law to compute F_N when the sled is moving horizontally and when the sled goes over the crest. The top diagram shows the forces on the child when the sled is moving horizontally. The acceleration a is 0, so the net force on the child is 0, and therefore, $F_N = Mg$.

The bottom diagram shows the forces on the child when the sled goes over the crest of the hill. There are two factors that reduce F_N in this situation; (a) the child now has centripetal acceleration in a direction opposite to the normal force, and (b) the weight (the local force of gravity) is no longer along the same axis as the normal force, so only the component $Mg \cos \theta$ is opposite in direction to F_N. If we choose the positive y-axis as the direction of F_N, then the y-component of the net force is

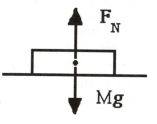

     $F_y = F_N - Mg \cos \theta = - Mv^2/R.$
Therefore,

     $F_N = Mg \cos \theta - Mv^2/R.$

16.   The satellite is kept up by its tangential speed. Although the satellite is constantly falling towards Earth, its tangential speed is such that it follows Earth's curvature and just keeps going round and round because its centripetal acceleration equals its gravitational acceleration.

17.   When the runner has both feet off the ground, there is no upward force on him and he is in free fall and, therefore, weightless.

18.   If its orbital speed is greater in winter, Earth must be closer to the Sun in winter. The effect of this on the seasons is overwhelmed by the 23° tilt of Earth's axis with respect to the normal to its orbital plane. (Note: This problem is guilty of northern-hemispheric-centrism. When it is winter in the northern hemisphere, it is of course summer in the southern hemisphere.)

Chapter 6

1.   In physics, work is defined as the product of force times the displacement of the object in the direction that the force points. In everyday language this corresponds to physical work or labor, but does not encompass "intellectual work."

2.   For an object traveling in a circle, the centripetal force does no work because the displacement (along the tangent) is always perpendicular to the direction of the centripetal force. Work is done by the centripetal force if the object is displaced radially by the centripetal force: positive work if the object is displaced radially inwards and negative work if the object is displaced radially outwards. For example, the orbits of the planets are ellipses and the gravitational force of the Sun does positive work on the planets during the part of the orbit where the distance from the Sun is decreasing and negative work on the planets during the part of the orbit where the distance from the Sun is increasing.

3.   Consider the following example. A person is standing in an elevator. If the elevator is at rest, the force exerted on the person by the elevator floor is called a *normal force* (it is a contact force perpendicular to the common solid surface). What if the elevator is moving up or down (with $\vec{a} = 0$, to make it simple)? Shouldn't the force of the elevator floor on the person still be called a normal force? Since the person moves parallel to this force (if the elevator is going up) or anti-parallel (if the elevator is going down), this is a case in which the normal force does do work on the person.

Jumping vertically (e.g., on a trampoline) is another example in which the person moves parallel to the direction of the normal force and work is done by the normal force.

4.   a) Yes, she is exerting a force on the water and moving some water in the direction that she exerts the force.
        b) During the change from swimming to floating, the water is exerting a force on her in the direction that she moves, and thus, the water does work on her. If she then floats along with the current at a constant velocity relative to the shore, the water exerts no force on her (if air resistance is zero), and thus, the net force on her is zero. Therefore, the net work done on her by the water is zero.

5.   No. As indicated in the hint, sometimes the friction force is in the same direction as the displacement and hence does positive work.

6.   You do no work on the wall but work *is* being done within your arm as your muscle fibers contract; when you exert a force on another object, small continual motions in your muscles get you tired. With your arm extended away from your body, try holding a lighted flashlight still in your hand and you will see the result of the small motions in your muscles.

7.   Take $k_1 > k_2$. In magnitude, the applied force equals the spring force $F = kx$.
        a) With $F_1 = F_2$, then $x_2 > x_1$ (i.e., spring 2 will stretch more) and $W_2 = Fx_2 > W_1 = Fx_1$.

        b) If they are stretched the same distance, then, since $W = PE = \frac{1}{2}kx^2$, $W_1 > W_2$.

8.   Since both m and v^2 are always positive, $KE = \frac{1}{2}mv^2$ is always positive.

Chapter 6

9.   Since force is constant, acceleration is constant and speed will change by equal amounts in equal time intervals. Since it starts at rest and reaches v_B a distance d away after a time Δt, it will take less than Δt to go the same distance from B to C, since it starts out with speed v_B. Since the time interval from B to C is less, the change in v will be less and final v_C will be less than 2 v_B.

Let us apply the work-energy principle, which is $W_{net} = \Delta KE$. Since the force is constant and $W_{net} = F_{net}\,\Delta x$, it requires twice as much work to move the block from A to C as to move it from A to B. Starting from rest, the block then has twice as much kinetic energy at C as it has at B. Since KE is defined as $\frac{1}{2}Mv^2$, increasing the KE by a factor of 2 will increase v by a factor of $2^{1/2}$, so $v_C = 2^{1/2}\,v_B$; thus, v_C is greater than v_B but less than 2 v_B.

10. $\Delta PE = Mgh$. Let $M = 85$ kg, $g = 9.8$ m/s^2 and $h = 0.75$ m; then $\Delta PE = 625$ joules.

11.   The situation shown violates conservation of energy. To get the water to flow up to the top again, work must be done on the water. There is nothing shown in the diagram to do the required work against the force of gravity. The illusion is accomplished by placing certain columns in physically impossible positions. Escher drew different parts of the picture for different perspectives.

12.   Using conservation of energy, writing v_0 for initial speed, v for final speed, and h for height of building, and setting the gravitational potential energy to be equal to zero at street level, we have $\frac{1}{2}mv_0^2 + mgh = \frac{1}{2}mv^2$, giving $v = (v_0^2 + 2gh)^{1/2}$. Neglecting air resistance, all the water balloons will have the same speed at impact.

13.   Using conservation of energy, at the highest point, h_{max}, (which occurs at the largest angle), the KE = 0 and $0 + mgh_{max} = \frac{1}{2}mv^2 + mgh$. Since v enters as the square, the direction is irrelevant, and the pendulum's maximum angle will be the same in both cases.

14.   A certain amount of work, depending on the force constant, must be done to compress a spring a distance Δx. This work goes into elastic potential energy, while gravitational potential energy decreases. When the spring is released (assuming that you can get your hand away quickly enough or have some way of keeping the spring temporarily compressed), some of the stored elastic potential energy is transformed into gravitational potential energy and kinetic energy (and some elastic potential energy). If the elastic potential energy when compressed is sufficiently greater than the decrease in gravitational potential energy, the spring (and whatever is attached) should bounce up. It is the comparison of elastic and gravitational potential energies that is crucial. Experimentally, the common springs we used did not support themselves, fell over, and could not be used to demonstrate this effect. A widely-sold toy has the spring enclosed in a plastic housing, does work this way, and jumps up from the surface when released.

15.   If he just lets it go, the initial total energy equals the gravitational potential energy and that ensures that the bowling ball will swing back to his nose and no farther. If he pushes the ball away, he adds KE to the potential energy to make a larger total energy than the initial total energy; that additional energy will mess up his face when the ball returns.

16.   The PE changes to KE, which then is dissipated in creating waves and splashes (i.e., some of it goes back temporarily into PE) and eventually goes into thermal energy, or, if the pool has an outlet, into the KE of the moving water.

17.   When the child first jumps on the pogo stick, the spring is compressed and the gravitational potential energy and kinetic energy are converted to elastic potential energy. While the spring extends, this energy is converted to gravitational PE and KE. At full extension, KE = 0 and energy is stored as gravitational PE plus elastic PE, assuming the spring is extended beyond its equilibrium length. The cycle then repeats.

18.   Gravitational PE changes to KE, which is dissipated into work and heat in messing up the snowbank (and possibly the skier).

19.   The question should refer to the speed, not the velocity, at the bottom, since the direction of the velocity does depend on the angle.

        a) In the absence of friction, the equation of conservation of mechanical energy implies that the speed is independent of the angle and equal to that acquired in falling a distance h.

        b) If there is friction, the speed at the bottom depends on the distance the sled slides along the plane and, thus, depends on the angle (some energy is converted into thermal energy via friction.)

20.   Stepping on top of the log requires that work be done to raise your mass against gravity to the height of the log. In jumping down, you hit the ground with greater force and can twist your ankle. In stepping over the log, you raise a smaller mass (i.e., your foot and leg) so it requires less work, and your horizontal motion continues without interruption.

21.   a) The kinetic energy comes from conversion of chemical energy into thermal energy when the fuel is burned, and as the hot gas expands, this energy is partially converted into the kinetic energy that turns the crankshaft. The work that produces the change in the kinetic energy of the car is done by the expanding gases that push on the piston to turn the crankshaft.

        b) In accelerating, the tires push back on the road and the road pushes forward on the tires. As pointed out in Section 5-3, when the tires are rolling, the bottom of the tire is at rest relative to the road. Therefore, the road does no work on the tires (see Section 8-7 for further discussion of this point); the car takes no energy from the road. The force of static friction does limit how fast the car can accelerate since to avoid skidding, the contact region between tire and road must be at rest.

22.   We may solve by applying the work-energy principle, $W_{net} = \Delta KE$. Since the displacement of the arrow is opposite in direction to the frictional force F_f, the net work is $W_{net} = -F_f\, x$. Since the arrow ends up at rest, $\Delta KE = -\frac{1}{2}M v_0^2$. If arrow 2 has twice the initial speed of arrow 1, it will have 4 times the initial kinetic energy, so 4 times as much work will be required to stop it. Since F_f is the same for both arrows, arrow 2 will penetrate 4 times as far.

In terms of Newton's Laws, a constant frictional force means a constant (negative) acceleration. We can then apply Newton's Second Law as $a = F_f/m = \Delta v/\Delta t$; for $v_2 = 2\, v_1$, we find $\Delta v_2 = 2\, \Delta v_1$ [implying that the average speeds have to be related the same way, $v_{2,av} = 2\, v_{1,av}$] and $\Delta t_2 = 2\, \Delta t_1$, so $\Delta x_2 = v_{2,av}\, \Delta t_2 = 2\, v_{1,av}\, 2\Delta t_1 = 4\, \Delta x_1$, and an arrow having twice the speed has four times the penetration distance.

23.   a) If there is no friction, the gravitational PE at the top of the swing changes to KE at the bottom, which enables the pendulum to swing equally high on the other side, at which point all the KE has changed to PE. Then the cycle repeats.

         b) With friction, some gravitational PE of the pendulum is converted to thermal energy with each swing, and the amplitude gradually decreases. A pendulum clock would eventually stop. In a grandfather clock, there is a mechanism to replace the energy lost to friction. When the clock is wound up, weights are raised, providing gravitational PE. As the weights slowly descend, this energy is transferred to the pendulum to keep its amplitude constant.

24.   No. That would violate conservation of energy.

25.   a) No. It depends only on the difference in height between final and initial positions.
         b) No.
         c) Yes.
         d) Yes.

26.   Since power is the rate of doing work, the answer to (b) would change to yes.

27.   It enables you to do the work necessary to climb the mountain over a longer period of time and, therefore, the power you supply is less.

28.   Disregarding friction losses, for every meter the load is raised, two meters of rope must be pulled up. Since the work done is the force times the distance through which the force is exerted, and since the pulley exerts twice the force on the piano that the person exerts on the rope, and since the work done on the piano must be the same as the work done by the man, conservation of energy requires that the man exerts his force over twice the distance the pulley moves the piano.

Chapter 7

1. The objects we observe are not in a closed system. They have a net external force acting on them. Momentum conservation holds only in isolated systems. In such a system no net force from outside the system acts on the system.

2. It is transferred to the whole Earth.

3. When you release an inflated untied balloon the balloon acquires a momentum equal and opposite that of the escaping gas, because the total (zero) momentum of the initial system must be conserved. [One may also discuss this question as an application of Newton's Third Law, but for this chapter, the emphasis is on the momentum approach.]

4. He should have thrown the coins as hard as he could in the direction away from the nearest shore. Momentum conservation would then give him a velocity towards the shore. In a truly frictionless environment (no air resistance, etc.) throwing a single coin should do it.

5. The rocket can change direction by emitting a jet of gas in the opposite direction. Conservation of momentum will then impart momentum to the rocket in the desired direction.

6. When a car hits a brick wall or is in a head-on collision with an oncoming car, its momentum is reduced to zero in a very short time, as is the momentum of the people inside. Heads go through windshields, chests are crushed by steering wheels, etc. Extremely large forces act for very short times to provide the impulse necessary to reduce the momentum to zero. If airbags deploy, the momentum is brought to zero in a much longer time and a correspondingly smaller force is exerted, minimizing damage to the occupants.

7. Crumple zones make the collision more inelastic and reduce the severity of the forces during the collision by increasing the time during which the forces act. If the crumple zones are properly designed, the kinetic energy of the collision is dissipated in collapsing these zones without crumpling the passengers.

8. A ball tossed in the air by the batter has little or no velocity in the horizontal direction, while a pitched ball's velocity is primarily horizontal and will make an elastic collision with the bat and reverse direction even if the bat is held still. If the bat is swung at the incoming ball, its momentum can be increased considerably, increasing the probability of hitting a home run.

9. The ball makes what is essentially an elastic collision with the racket and reverses direction. See question 8 above dealing with a baseball and bat.

10. Since impulse $= \vec{F} \Delta t$, a small force F applied for a sufficiently long time interval Δt can result in a larger impulse than a large force applied for a short time interval. This is the principle of "solar sailing" (using the impulse imparted by sunlight on huge sails for interplanetary travel).

11. $M > m$. If $\frac{1}{2}MV_M^2 = \frac{1}{2}mv_m^2$, then $MV_M = (Mm)^{1/2} v_m > mv_m$. The more massive body has the greater momentum.

12.   The total (linear) momentum of an object is the momentum of the center of mass.

An object cannot have momentum without having kinetic energy, since momentum $= m\vec{v}$ and $KE = \frac{1}{2}mv^2$. If the CM of the object has nonzero v, then the CM will have both momentum and kinetic energy. If the CM has $v = 0$, then the total momentum of the object is zero and the kinetic energy of the CM is zero. An object that is a point mass will have no kinetic energy if its momentum is zero. However, if the object is extended, then (even though the CM has zero velocity) the object could be rotating and, thus, have rotational kinetic energy about the CM or KE associated with expansion or vibration relative to the CM. Thus, an extended object can have kinetic energy with a total momentum of zero.

13.   They should be designed so that the water rebounds, because that would impart more momentum to the blades.

14.   a) No. Since it is accelerating downward, its momentum is constantly increasing. When it rebounds, its momentum is reversed and as it rises it is still accelerating downward with its momentum decreasing.

        b) In the case of the Earth-ball system, momentum is conserved throughout since, (if we neglect the gravitational forces exerted by other astronomical bodies) no net external force acts on the system.

        c) Same as for part b).

15.   To maintain balance, you need to keep your CM directly above your feet; otherwise the force of gravity acting on your CM will cause you to tip over. (This issue will be treated in more detail in Section 9-5.) If you did not lean backwards, then adding the heavy load to your arms in front of you would shift the center of mass forward.

16.   The pipe is uniform, so its CM is at its midpoint. Arms and legs are not uniform cylinders, but have more mass closer to the body than at the extremities. Hence, their CM is displaced towards the more massive regions.

17.

18.   Use geometry. Draw a line from a vertex so that it bisects opposite side. This divides the triangle into two triangles of equal area. (Recall that the area of a triangle equals one-half the altitude times the base. The two triangles have the same altitude and the bases were made equal.) The CM must lie on this line. Repeat this process using a second vertex. The CM must be the point at which the two lines intersect. Doing it with the third vertex is not necessary. Its line will also go through the CM.

19.   The CM of the system of pieces will continue to follow the original path. All the forces involved in the explosion were internal to the system and, therefore, the momentum of the system was unchanged.

20.   The engine rotates the driving wheels, whose tires exert a backward frictional force on the road and by Newton's Third Law, the road exerts a forward force on the driving wheels. This is the external force that accelerates the car.

Chapter 8

1.   Since you don't have a device for measuring the angle θ in (a) directly, set up a right triangle in (b) that is similar to the right triangle in (a). With your arm extended in front of you, hold the meter stick vertically, adjust the level of the meter stick so that you sight along the top of the meter stick to the top of the statue, and then measure the vertical distance y from the top of the meter stick to your eye level. Next, measure the horizontal distance x that your arm was extended. You have now measured sides x, y of a right triangle similar to the one formed by the height h of the statue and the known distance D to it, so solve for h = D (y/x).

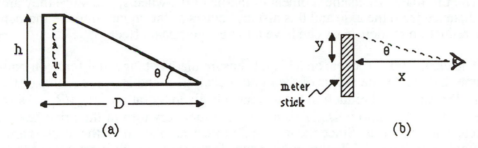

(a)   (b)

This actually gives the height of the statue above your eye level, so, as a small correction, you can add to h the height of your eye level.

2.   An odometer meant to be used for 27" diameter wheels is designed so that each revolution corresponds to the distance traveled of π(27"), but in fact you will be traveling only π(24"). Thus, the odometer will read high by a factor of 27/24. That is, it will read a distance traveled that is 12.5% too high.

3.   If a turntable rotates at constant angular velocity, a point on the rim has radial (centripetal) acceleration but no tangential acceleration. If the turntable accelerates, the point will have both radial and tangential acceleration. If the angular acceleration is uniform, the magnitude of the radial acceleration would change, but that of the tangential acceleration would not.

4.   Since both sides of the equation would be multiplied by the same conversion factor to convert degrees to radians, Equations 8-9 would not have to be altered.

5.   Since $|\tau| = |r|\ |F| \sin \theta$, i.e., torque equals product of force times lever arm, a small force can exert a greater torque than a larger force if r sin θ is large enough.

6.   If force acts on a body with zero lever arm, it will not produce a torque but will add to the net force on the body and produce a change in its motion. (i.e., does not produce an angular acceleration but can produce a linear acceleration.)

7.   Giancoli should have drawn a figure to show the initial position of the arms since the phrase "hands … outstretched in front of you," is not clear. One interpretation is that when you are initially lying on the floor, your arms point towards the ceiling. The other interpretation is that in your initial position, your arms point towards your toes. With the first interpretation, it is more difficult to do a sit-up from this position than with your arms folded behind your head, because the outstretched arms are farther from the pivot point and, thus, increase your moment of inertia relative to the pivot point. With the second interpretation, it is easier to do a sit-up from this position than with your arms folded behind your head because the outstretched arms are closer to the pivot point and thus,

7., continued

decrease your moment of inertia. In either case, the greater your moment of inertia relative to the pivot point, the greater the torque required to produce the same angular acceleration.

Interestingly, women tended to interpret the phrase "outstretched in front of you" differently from men, and neither side could convince the other.

8.   The tire mass affects the moment of inertia of the wheels, and since they are at the farthest distance from the axle and this distance enters as the square into the moment of inertia, a reduction in their mass can have a more significant effect.

9.   The chain and sprockets on a bicycle ensure that the tangential force on both gears is the same. Let R_{in} be the radius of the input (pedal) gear and R_{out} the radius of the output (rear wheel) gear. Speed reduction (or increase) is given by ratio of R_{out}/R_{in}. As an example, assume this ratio is 1/3. This means that for every turn of the drive gear, the output gear makes 3 turns. Since the tangential forces are the same, the torques are proportional to the radii, while the angular speeds are inversely proportional to the radii.

Therefore, assuming one wants a constant torque at the rear wheel, more torque must be applied to a given size pedal sprocket when the rear sprocket is small and less when it is large. Similarly, a large front sprocket requires more torque than a small one to deliver the same torque to a given size rear sprocket. In both cases, the bicycle will speed up if the pedaling speed remains constant.

This interplay between required torque at the rear wheel (as in going uphill), pedaling speed (which most bicyclists prefer to be as constant as possible), and rear wheel (bicycle) speed is complex, as might be suggested by the fact that there are 21 possible gear combinations.

10.   It minimizes the moment of inertia of the legs.

11.   Tightrope walkers carry a long, narrow beam to increase their stability and help them keep their footing. The long rods increase the moment of inertia of the tightrope walker about axes perpendicular to the rods. Also, shifting the position of the rods can be used to shift the center of mass of the tightrope walker.

12.   The net force on a system can be zero without the net torque being zero. Example: Two equal and opposite forces separated by a lever arm acting on an extended object. The net torque on a system can be zero without the net force being zero—see Question 8-6 above.

13.   The CM will fall straight down. The top end rotates down in the direction tipped as a result of the torque exerted by gravity, while the bottom end slides along the ground until the stick ends up horizontally on the ground.

14.   Speed at bottom is the same in both cases. Since the ball starts at the same height in both cases, it has the same initial PE in both cases, and thus, by conservation of mechanical energy, the ball will have the same total KE at the bottom for both inclines. Although the steep incline produces greater acceleration, it provides a shorter distance for attaining the final velocity.

15.	Applying conservation of mechanical energy at the top and the bottom of the incline:
$$Mgh = \frac{1}{2}Mv^2 + \frac{1}{2}I\omega^2.$$

Substituting $\omega = v/R$ and $I = \frac{2}{5}MR^2$ for the sphere gives

$$Mgh = (1 + \frac{2}{5})\frac{1}{2}Mv^2 = \frac{7}{10}Mv^2 = \text{total KE at the bottom.}$$

Therefore,
>	a) the speed at bottom is independent of mass and radius,
>	b) both reach the bottom at the same time, and
>	c) the total KE at the bottom is greater for the sphere with twice the mass and is
independent of radius.

16.	The sphere has the greater speed at the bottom and reaches the bottom first. The total KE at the bottom = PE at the top = Mgh, which is the same for both, since both have the same mass. The sphere has a smaller moment of inertia I than the cylinder. Since rotational $KE = \frac{1}{2}I\omega^2$, the cylinder will have the greater rotational KE and the smaller translational KE, which is why the sphere wins the race.

17.	The motion is a combination of both. The CM of the bicycle has translational motion along the path, while the bicycle slowly rotates about its CM with its front wheel higher on the upgrade, both wheels at the same height at the top and the front wheel lower than the rear wheels on the downgrade.

18.	Momentum and angular momentum are conserved only in isolated systems, which means no net forces (and hence no net torques) from outside the system act on it. The slowing down occurs because net external forces such as friction are acting on the system.

19.	This would increase the moment of inertia of Earth about its axis since more of its mass would be concentrated at the farthest distance from the axis. Since angular momentum $I\omega$ must be conserved in this isolated system, ω must decrease and the day would last longer than 24 hours.

20.	The diver needs some initial rotation (angular momentum) when she leaves the board. (The human body cannot manipulate its moment of inertia like a cat, which allegedly can impart opposite angular momenta to different portions of its body during a fall, enabling it to rotate and land on its feet.)

21.	Earth's angular velocity vector points north along its axis of rotation. (Use the right hand rule with fingers pointing from west to east in a counterclockwise sense as viewed from the north pole.)

22.	a) The linear velocity at top points into the page, which is north .

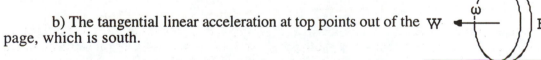

	b) The tangential linear acceleration at top points out of the page, which is south.

	c) It is decreasing, since angular acceleration is opposite to angular velocity.

23.   The front of the cycle rises up to conserve the angular momentum of the bike.

24.   As you walk toward the center of a rotating turntable, your tangential speed decreases, although your angular velocity remains the same. When you reach the center, your tangential speed becomes zero and you rotate about your vertical axis with the angular velocity of the turntable.

25.   While in the air, the only force acting on him is the downward force of gravity, which exerts no torque in the vertical direction. Therefore, the component of his angular momentum in the vertical direction must be conserved, so if he rotates his upper body in one direction, he must rotate his lower body in the opposite direction.

26.   The direction of the angular momentum of the second hand is into the face of the clock.

27.   Suppose the rotor speed increases while the helicopter is in the air. If the helicopter had only one rotor, the rest of it would have to spin in the opposite direction in order to conserve angular momentum. Using two rotors going in opposite directions, but both adjusted for lift, would avoid this. More commonly, a small propeller in the back, rotating in the vertical plane, keeps the cabin from spinning. Since the question referred to conservation of angular momentum, we are neglecting any possible torques exerted by the air on the helicopter.

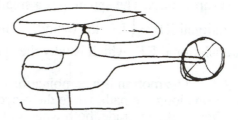

Chapter 9

1.   These are situations where the net force on the body is zero but the net torque is nonzero, so there is a nonzero angular acceleration, but the center of mass does not accelerate. Examples:

   a) two children of different weights climb onto the opposite ends of a see-saw.

   b) a gust of wind increases the angular velocity of a windmill.

   c) a record turntable is turned on.

2.   No. The bungee cord exerts an upward force greater than the downward force of his weight and he will accelerate upward. If he were in equilibrium, he would have remained where he was.

3.   The finger closer to the CG will support more of the weight of the stick (see Example 9-7) than the one farther away (on the other side) and, therefore, the perpendicular component of the force of the stick on the closer finger will be greater, causing friction to increase as well. Therefore, the finger farther away will be less subject to friction and hence more likely to slide, bringing it closer to the CG. Whichever finger is farther from the CG will slide closer to it, until both fingers meet there at the CG.

4.   The weights are linked with longer lever arms to the fulcrum or pivot than you are, so the torque you exert can be balanced by the torque exerted by the much smaller sliding weights. An analogy would be a see-saw with one end cut off, leaving just enough room for you to sit on. A small child sitting at the far end opposite could then balance the torque you exert.

5.   Consider forces on point P:

$T_1 = T_2 = T$,

$\Sigma F_y = 2T \cos \theta - Mg = 0$.

$$T = \frac{Mg}{2 \cos \theta}$$

As the pack rises, θ increases, $\cos \theta$ decreases, and the applied force T must increase. The rope will always sag, because for $\theta = 90°$, $\cos \theta = 0$, and T would be infinite.

6.   A ladder is more likely to slip when the person is near the top. This is easy to see if you take the pivot point where the ladder touches the ground. As the person moves up the ladder, the lever arm relative to this pivot point increases, so the person exerts a greater torque. The only force that exerts a torque in the opposite direction is the horizontal force of the wall on the ladder. To satisfy the first condition of equilibrium, the horizontal force of the wall on the ladder must equal in magnitude the frictional force exerted by the ground on the ladder. This frictional force has some maximum value, independent of any torques. If the horizontal force of the wall required to satisfy the torque equilibrium condition exceeds the maximum frictional force of the ground, the ladder will slip.

7.   In the standing position, the upper body is almost horizontal and the weights of the head, arms, and trunk are vertical. This produces large torques about the fulcrum. Also, since the back muscles act at an angle of only 12° relative to the spine, the force exerted on the vertebra must have a large horizontal component

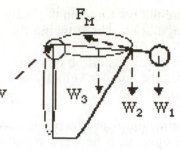

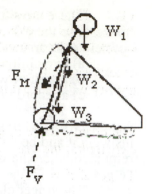

to maintain equilibrium. In the sitting position with legs extended, the trunk is more nearly vertical, i.e., more aligned with the weight of the upper body, thus, reducing the torques; the force exerted on the vertebra is reduced, particularly the horizontal component. The notation used is that of Fig. 9-16.

8.   a) Take pivot point P at the corner of the wall which is lowest as the wall just starts to tip. If the wall is tipping, then the force of friction F_f and the normal force F_N act at this point and have zero lever arm. If the center of mass of the wall is to the right of P, then the force of gravity on the wall exerts a torque opposite in direction to that of F_E, the horizontal force of the soil on the wall, and this keeps the wall upright.

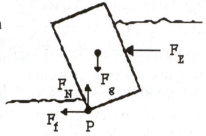

b) Adding the horizontal section of the wall has two effects that make the wall less likely to overturn. The soil above the horizontal part exerts a normal force F_{Ey} that produces a torque opposite to F_{Ex} (relative to the labeled pivot point P). Secondly, the CM is shifted to the right and down. This increases the lever arm of the gravitational torque on the wall opposite to the torque produced by F_{Ex}.

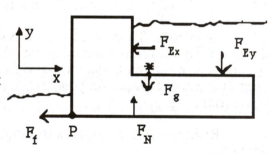

9.

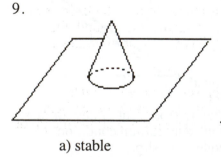

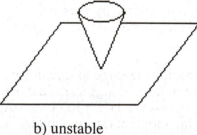

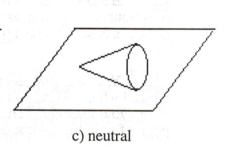

a) stable   b) unstable   c) neutral

10.   Since the mass of the uniform meter stick can be considered to be concentrated at the 50 cm mark, the fact that a support at the 25 cm mark balances the rock means that the mass of the meter stick equals that of the rock.

11.   First consider the simpler situation of a single brick extending over the edge of the table. The brick's center of gravity must be supported by the table;

otherwise the torque $\vec{\tau}_g$ acting on the brick's center of gravity will cause it to tip.

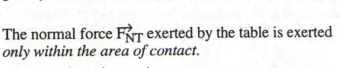
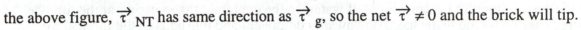

The normal force $\vec{F}_{NT}$ exerted by the table is exerted *only within the area of contact.*

To get $\Sigma\vec{\tau} = \vec{\tau}_g + \vec{\tau}_{NT}$, the table must be able to

exert a normal force along the line of action of $\vec{F}_g$. In

the above figure, $\vec{\tau}_{NT}$ has same direction as $\vec{\tau}_g$, so the net $\vec{\tau} \neq 0$ and the brick will tip.

For the situation in Figure 9-45, treat the 2 bricks as one system, and assume uniform bricks. In Fig 9-45a, only $\frac{3}{8}$ of the mass of the system is over the table, so the CG of the system is not over the table—it is not in equilibrium.

In Fig 9-45b, $\frac{1}{2}$ of the mass of the system is over the table, so the CG of the system lies above the edge of the table. This is an example of unstable equilibrium: if bricks are moved out slightly, they will fall.

12.   A. Unstable; B. Stable; C. Neutral

13.   See Ch. 7, Question 15. The heavy load acts to move the center of mass of you and the load forward. If this means that the CM is no longer over your feet (which are the base of support), the gravitational torque will make you fall forward. By leaning backward, you keep the center of mass over your feet so as to maintain the second condition of equilibrium.

14.   Rising on tiptoes requires shifting your CM forward. The door prevents you from doing that.

15.   Because in the sitting position your center of mass is above your buttocks instead of over your feet; as soon as you try to rise by pressing your feet against the ground, the ground's reaction force produces an unbalanced torque that makes you sit right down again.

16.   Your legs and feet provide the same torque in the opposite direction from that applied when you do a sit-up with your legs stretched out as when your knees are bent. When your knees are bent, you exert a larger force on your lower back just above the pivot point of your hips, because the moment arm is shorter.

17.   Yes, the two blades produce a shear stress at the cut.

18.   It could be used for the front support, which is under compression. It should not be used for the rear support, which would be under tension. (This assumes that some means is provided to fasten the beam to the support.)

Chapter 10

1.   Not necessarily. The molecules may be spaced closer together so that there are more of them in a given volume. For example, gold has a higher density than lead, but an atom of lead has more mass than an atom of gold.

2.   Lowered air pressure in the airplane cabin can cause these leaks. If the containers were filled near sea level, the inside will be at a higher pressure than the outside and force some of the fluid out. Even modern pressurized cabin and cargo holds are not pressurized to sea level pressure but slightly less; the change in pressure becomes noticeable in your ears as the airplane descends.

3.   Recall that the hydrostatic force is everywhere perpendicular to the walls. In the cylindrical vessel, therefore, the walls do not exert any vertical reaction force. However, in the container that is wider at the top, the walls exert a force having an upward component and, thus, support the extra weight of water. In the container that narrows at the top, the force exerted by the walls has a downward component and this adds to the force at the base.

4.   The pressure. The end of the pin has a much smaller area than the blunt end of the pen and, thus, exerts a greater pressure given the same force.

5.   If a number of vessels of various shapes are interconnected and open to the same atmospheric pressure, water poured into them will rise to the same level in each, since the water pressure at depth h is $P = P_0 + \rho gh$, and so must be the same in each vessel when the fluid is at rest.

6.   After the water boils in the can, the can is filled with water vapor (steam). As the vapor cools, its pressure decreases, and since the lid keeps air from entering and equalizing the pressure, atmospheric pressure eventually crushes the can.

7.   The siphon requires atmospheric pressure for its operation. It is atmospheric pressure that forces the liquid uphill (so long as height $< \frac{P_{atm}}{\rho g}$ where ρ is density of the liquid). The reason that the liquid on each side stays up is that the pressure in the tube is lower than atmospheric, and so the atmospheric pressure on the liquid surfaces forces the liquid to stay in the tube.

8.   No. The density of ice is less than that of water. When the ice is floating, the submerged portion displaces a volume of water equal in weight to the ice cube. The volume of water produced by the completely melted ice just fills the volume that was taken up by the submerged portion of the ice cube. Thus, the water level does not change.

9.   An ice cube will not float in a glass of alcohol because ice is denser than alcohol. Therefore, the buoyant force upward on the ice cube is less than its weight and it will sink.

10.   We shall assume that sand covers the full area of the barge at a uniform height h_s above the deck. Removing sand would decrease the weight of water displaced by the barge by the amount $\rho_s g A \Delta h_s = \rho_w g A \Delta h_b$, where Δh_s is the decrease in the height of sand above the deck and where Δh_b is the increase in the height of the barge above the water. Making the reasonable assumption that sand is denser than water, we see that $\Delta h_b > \Delta h_s$ and thus, there is a net gain in height, and passage under the bridge becomes even more difficult.

Conversely, if a certain height of sand is added, the barge will sink by a greater amount and might be able to clear the bridge.

11.   In version (a) of this answer, we assume that the balloon has strong, rigid sides and cannot expand. In version (b), we treat, instead, a rubber balloon but then we need to use Avogadro's hypothesis from Chapter 13.
    a) A balloon with strong, rigid sides: (This approximations a certain type of weather balloon once it is fully expanded.) Air pressure and air density decrease with increasing altitude. As long as the weight of the air displaced by the balloon exceeds the weight of the balloon, there will be a net upwards force on the balloon. At some altitude, the density of the air will be sufficiently low, so that the weight of the displaced air equals the weight of the balloon. Above this altitude there is a net downwards force on the balloon, so this is the maximum altitude. Since the sides are strong and rigid, the air pressure on the outside of the balloon does not have to equal the pressure of the helium on the inside.

    b) A rubber balloon, such as one might buy at a carnival: The air pressure on the outside and the pressure of the helium on the inside must be equal; otherwise the balloon will either expand or collapse. As the balloon rises, the air pressure outside decreases, so the balloon expands. We compare the weight of the volume of air displaced by the balloon with the weight of the balloon when the pressure inside equals the pressure outside. According to Avogadro's hypothesis, equal volumes of gas at the same pressure and temperature contain the same number of molecules.

Since air molecules are heavier than helium molecules, the buoyant force will continue to exceed the weight of the balloon as the balloon continues to rise and expand. In practice, at some height (which is not very large for carnival balloons), the required expansion overstretches the balloon and the balloon will burst.

12.   Yes. The balloon filled with air will have a buoyant force equal to the weight of the air it displaces, which is the same as the weight of the air inside it.

13.   It should be greater, since water deep in the ocean is somewhat denser than that near the surface, because it is more compressed due to the enormous pressure at great depths.

14.   a) The level will fall when the boat is removed, since the volume of the submerged portion of boat will be missing.
    b) The level will fall because a volume of water equal in weight to the iron anchor is no longer displaced.
    c) The level will fall, but less than in (b) because a volume of water equal to the volume of the (denser) anchor is still displaced. Note that in this case, the anchor is not floating, but drops to the bottom of the pool. Thus, the volume of water displaced is equal to the volume of the anchor rather than a volume of water equal to the weight of the anchor, as is true when the anchor is in the boat.

15.   Since these balloons rise to high altitudes where the air pressure is considerably less than at ground level, and one wants the pressure inside to be in equilibrium with the lower pressure outside at the high altitude, one puts in just enough gas on the ground to fully inflate the balloon into a nice round sphere at the high altitude.

16.   Salt water is denser. Then, since $F_B = \rho_F g V$, where ρ_F is the density of the fluid and V is the volume submerged, you are supported by the same buoyant force in salt water with less of you submerged.

17.   If the measurement is not made at the level of the heart, you would need to correct for the difference in pressure $\Delta P = \rho g h$.

18.   The strong winds passing over the roof reduce the pressure just above it and the higher pressure inside the house blows it off.

19.   They will come together. By Bernoulli's principle, when you blow between the papers, the speed of the air increases and the pressure between them drops relative to the pressure outside, and so the papers are forced together.

20.   Bernoulli's principle states that pressure is reduced when air is moving rapidly. The air is moving rapidly over the canvas convertible top of the moving car and the differential pressure between the moving air outside and the still air inside causes the top to bulge outward.

21.   Yes. The Bernoulli effect causes a decrease in pressure near the train, which produces a force toward the train acting on people standing close. Because of friction, the air near the train moves at about the speed of the train and, therefore, has a nonzero velocity with respect to the air farther away.

22.   a) A keel is necessary for sailing into the wind. With proper maneuvering, the force on the sails can be made perpendicular to the wind direction. This force, added to the reaction force of the water on the keel, has a resultant opposite to the wind direction. (See Fig. 10-24 (d).)

        b) At anchor, a boat should float freely at the surface. A keel could produce undesirable forces and torques in response to any disturbance or motion of the water.

23.   No. In free fall, effective g is zero and so there will be no pressure difference between the top and bottom of the water in the cup and the flow would stop.

24.   Because of the Bernoulli effect, the high speed air reduces the pressure above the dime enough to let the normal pressure on the underside pick it up. (Note that there is air between the bottom face of the dime and the table because of the sculpted surface.)

25.   The lift of the wings depends on the motion of the air relative to the wings. Taking off into the wind enables a plane to get into the air in a shorter distance while using less fuel, since the wind contributes "free" relative motion.

26.   In normal flight, hummingbirds gain lift from the motion of the air over their wings, similar to an airplane. When hovering, they must produce all the lift with rapid motions of their wings. This requires more energy.

27.   As the water falls, it gains speed, and by friction makes the air near it move along. This moving air causes the pressure surrounding the stream to drop by Bernoulli's principle, and the higher pressure air outside squeezes the water so that it moves as a stream.

One may deduce the narrowing of the stream of falling water directly from the equation of continuity: $A_1v_1 = A_2v_2$. Since v increases as the water falls, the cross sectional area A will decrease.

28.   At Earth's surface, the friction between the air and the ground resists movement of the air relative to the ground, and the viscosity of the air propagates this tendency. The higher up we go, the freer the air is to move and the greater is the average wind speed.

The mole takes advantage of this when it builds its burrow with one entrance higher than the other, because the greater wind speed at the higher end produces a lowered pressure by the Bernoulli principle, which causes air to flow through the burrow and ventilate it.

29.   Water is less viscous at 40 °C than at 20 °C, making the drag force on the ball bearing less at 40 °C than at 20 °C. This means the bearing will reach the bottom more quickly at 40 °C.

Chapter 11

1.   Examples of vibrating objects: a rocking chair in motion, your vocal chords, a plucked guitar string, the surface of a pond after a stone is thrown in, a tuning fork that has been struck, wings of flying insects or humming birds, tree branches moving up and down in the wind.

Most of these exhibit approximate SHM until friction decreases the amplitude of the vibration and the vibration stops, or an external driving force (for example, the wind in the case of the tree branch) causes a change in the vibration. The tuning fork's vibration is sinusoidal and, thus, aside from damping, is a good example of SHM. The vibrations of the vocal chords and the plucked guitar string are a combination of several simple harmonic motions with different frequencies present at the same time (see Section 12-6), but for the guitar string, one of these simple harmonic motions dominates.

2.   A SHO has $\vec{a} = 0$ when it passes through its equilibrium position.

3.   The piston in an automobile engine does not move in SHM because the force (and therefore, the acceleration) is greater when the air-fuel mixture ignites at one end of the maximum displacement than it is on the other, where it is coasting. Assuming the pistons are properly timed, the more cylinders an engine has, the closer the motions will approximate SHM and the smoother the engine will run.

4.   The spring can be considered to contribute some of its mass to the mass on the end, and since $T = 2\pi(m/k)^{1/2}$, where m is the mass at the end of a weightless spring, the period of a real spring will be greater. Since $f = \frac{1}{T}$, the frequency will be smaller.

5.   Since the maximum speed is ωA, where $\omega = 2\pi f$ and A is the amplitude, doubling A will double the maximum speed.

6.   The car-and-spring system can be thought of as a mass and spring combination. The period of this system is given by $T = 2\pi (m/k)^{1/2}$. Denote the mass of the empty car by m, and the loaded car by $m + \mu$; then the period for the loaded car is
$$T_{loaded} = 2\pi ([m + \mu]/k)^{1/2} > T_{unloaded} = 2\pi (m/k)^{1/2}.$$
This means that the bouncing takes longer (i.e., it is slower).

7.   a) f is independent of amplitude A.

b) $v_{max} = (k/m)^{1/2}A$, so if amplitude doubles, the maximum velocity doubles.

c) $a_{max} = (k/m) A$, so if amplitude doubles, maximum acceleration doubles.

d) $E = \frac{1}{2} kA^2$, so if amplitude doubles, total mechanical energy increases by a factor of 4.

8. $T = 2\pi(L/g)^{1/2}$. At high altitude g will be slightly smaller, T will increase, and the pendulum clock will lose time.

9.   The tire is connected to the branch by a rope of length L. The system is close to an ideal pendulum, and the ideal pendulum of length L has a period $T = 2\pi(L/g)^{1/2}$. Measure the time for 10 periods (to decrease errors) with the stopwatch. Divide by 10 to get a measurement of T. Our resulting estimate for the branch's height is $L = g(T/2\pi)^2$.

10.   This is a resonance phenomenon similar to pushing a child on a swing. You must push the swing (or shake the pan) at the right time, that is, with a frequency equal to one of the natural frequencies of the system, to keep up the oscillations. For example, if you shake the pan with a period equal to the round trip time for the water wave to travel to the opposite side and back, your shaking will be in phase with the wave and, by the principle of superposition, a large amplitude wave will result.

11.   This is an example of resonance: a response of large amplitude when the driving frequency is close to a natural frequency of f_0 of the system. The 264 Hz fork generates a 264 Hz sound wave which strikes the other 2 forks. The driving frequency = (frequency of incoming sound wave) = 264 Hz. This sound wave sets the 260 Hz fork into vibration because the natural frequency f_0 = 260 Hz of this fork differs by only

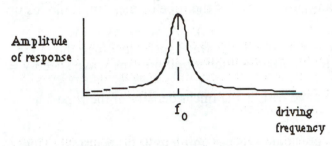

4 Hz from the driving frequency f. The driving frequency is too far from the natural frequency of the 420 Hz fork to excite any significant response.

12.   a) A child pumping a swing at its natural frequency.
       b) An unbalanced washing machine undergoes large vibrations and walks during the spin cycle.
       c) Blowing over a soda bottle to excite a note.
       d) If earthquake waves have frequency close to one of the natural frequencies of the buildings, the buildings are more likely to collapse (e.g., the Mexico City earthquake)

13.   Most rattles in cars are resonance phenomena caused by loose components resonating either to the engine vibration or to the motion of the car on the road. If the rattle occurs when the car is at rest with the engine running, it is the former; if it occurs only when the car is moving, it is the latter, for example the vibration may be excited by driving over a pot hole.

14.   Taking the natural frequency as $(2\pi)^{-1}(k/m)^{1/2}$, one sees that reducing the mass of the building will increase its natural frequency. Steel is stronger than stone and even though steel is denser, the total mass of a steel-framed building is less than that of a stone building of the same dimensions. The spring constant k is proportional to the elastic modulus (Young's modulus), which is greater for steel than for granite (see the Table in Section 9-6). Replacing a granite building with a steel-framed building of the same size increases the spring constant and decreases the mass, and so increases the natural frequency. This may make the natural frequency of the building closer to the vibration frequencies caused by passing trucks, etc., and thus, increase the problems with resonance.

15.   Yes, the frequency of the wave is the same as the frequency of vibration of the source. The bit of the medium next to the source gets "shaken" by the source at the frequency of the source: the bit of medium goes through one cycle in the same time it takes the source to complete one cycle. This bit of the medium now acts as a source to shake the next bit of the medium at the same frequency. Provided that the source remains at the same place in the medium (is not traveling through the medium), the wave disturbance at position x = vt from the source shows what the source was doing t seconds ago. [The hedge is because of the Doppler effect.]

16.   The wave speed is the speed at which energy is carried forward by the wave. Take a horizontal rope and shake one end up and down so that a sinusoidal wave travels along the rope with wave
velocity $\vec{v}$. As the disturbance passes any tiny portion of the rope of mass m, it moves up and down in SHM so that its speed varies from $v_{max} = (k/m)^{1/2}A$, where A is the amplitude of the vibration, to 0. If the rope is uniform, the wave speed at which the disturbance propagates is constant, and for small amplitude vibrations, the wave speed v = $\left(\frac{F_T}{M/L}\right)^{1/2}$. Here, F_T is the rope tension and M/L is the linear density of the rope.

17.   By wrapping the string, one increases the mass per unit length of the string. Since the speed of a wave on the string is v = $\left(\frac{F_T}{M/L}\right)^{1/2}$ and the fundamental frequency is f = v/2L, this decreases the wave speed and the fundamental frequency. The piano strings are wrapped with wire instead of simply making the steel string thicker so that they don't become too stiff.

18.   a) Transverse
        b) Longitudinal

19.   For a longitudinal wave in a fluid, $v = (B/\rho)^{1/2}$. Since the density ρ decreases as temperature increases, the speed of sound will increase as the temperature increases.

20.   a) The same amount of energy has to be distributed over a larger circumference. Since energy is proportional to the square of the amplitude, the amplitude must decrease as the circular waves move away from the source.

        b) Some of the energy is lost due to friction as the water moves. This goes into heating the water.

21.   Since energy is proportional to square of frequency in two otherwise identical waves, the one having half the wavelength of the other will have twice the frequency and will transmit four times the energy.

22.   When a sinusoidal wave crosses the boundary between two sections of rope, the frequency remains constant because at the boundary, the frequency of the incident wave ("jiggling") forces an oscillation of the transmitted wave with the same frequency.

22., continued

If the 2 sections of rope vibrated at different frequencies, the rope would probably break at the boundary!

23.   Waves obey the principle of superposition; classically, particles do not. So the most convincing evidence that the energy was being carried by waves would be to find interference effects. Waves can diffract around obstacles but particles do not, so place an obstacle in the path and see if diffraction occurs. [In the chapters on modern physics, we shall find that particles, especially those of atomic dimensions or smaller, display wave properties of interference and diffraction.]

24.   When a wave bends (diffracts) around an obstacle, the waves move into the "shadow" region somewhat (see the pictures on p. 339). The extent to which this happens is governed by the relative size of the obstacle and the wavelength of the wave: you get a well-defined shadow only if the obstacle is large compared with the wavelength. In this example, a hill is large compared to the radio wavelengths used for FM broadcasting, roughly 3 m. However, a hill is not large compared to the longer wavelengths used for AM reception, typically 200 to 600 m. So a hill casts a shadow for FM reception, but much less so for AM reception.

25.   A string which is vibrating in three segments has two nodes (in addition to the ends of the string) at which the string

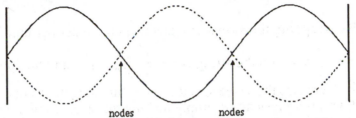

nodes   nodes

is not vibrating. You can touch the string with a knife blade at these points without disturbing the motion, because there is no transverse motion at these points.

26.   The wave energy is not destroyed. In a standing wave, the incident and reflected waves pass through one another in opposite directions without changing each other, and without loss of energy (see case of pulses in sketch below). The displacement of the string from equilibrium at any instant is the sum of the displacements of the two traveling waves (superposition); at a node, the two waves happen always to add to zero. But energy is still passing through the node in opposite directions, even though the displacement is zero there.

26., continued

For 2 pulses traveling in opposite directions with the same amplitude on the string, one has the situation shown in the diagram below.

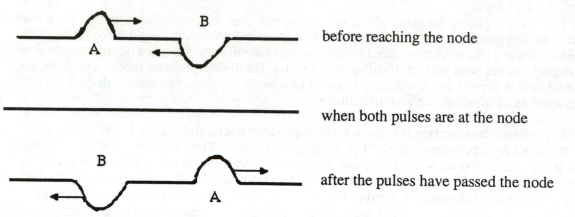

before reaching the node

when both pulses are at the node

after the pulses have passed the node

The pulses A and B do not stop at the node; there is no change in speed.

Chapter 12

1.   The most convincing evidence for wave behavior (as opposed to particle behavior) is interference effects, particularly those in which two waves add up (superimpose) to give zero. Two examples of interference effects with sound are:
      a) "dead" spots in a room or concert hall (standing waves);
      b) beats.

2.   Sound is a form of energy because it can do work. Sound can exert forces that set air or solid matter into vibratory motion. In extreme cases, it can cause damage as in "sonic booms," which can shatter windows and produce damage to windows.

3.   The sound wave that enters the cup on the left causes the paper on the cup bottom to vibrate. The string, attached to the cup bottom, vibrates with it. The string is tight, so the vibrations in the string travel along it and get to the other cup bottom. The string's vibrations cause the paper bottom of the cup on the right to move, which pushes the air in the cup into motion (creating a sound wave), which then moves as a sound wave to the waiting ear. This is effective because the sound energy is channeled along the string instead of spreading out in three dimensions.

4.   See Question 22 from Ch. 11. When a wave passes from one medium to another, the vibration of the first medium acts a source of vibration in the second medium. At the boundary, adjoining bits of the two media (here, air and water) must go through one cycle of vibration in the same time (one period), hence have the same frequency. The wavelength, on the other hand, is the distance a wave travels in one period. This depends on the velocity of waves in the material, which is in general different for different media. So the frequency is the same, but the wavelengths are in general different.

5.   The fact that sounds from distant sources do not seem distorted shows that v does not depend on f. Almost everything we hear is composed of a mixture of frequencies, and if they arrived at slightly different times, we would detect extreme distortion. Yet we can still understand someone shouting from a distance, or amplified sound from a remote bullhorn or loudspeaker, whether it be speech or music.

6.   Speech is produced by various membranes, cavities, etc., in the head and throat. The geometry of these speech-producing organs is independent of whether one has inhaled helium or air. Since it is the geometry that determines the wavelength, the relation $f = v/\lambda$ implies that f will be greater for helium because the speed of sound in helium is about three times that in air. The natural frequencies of vibration of one's vocal cavities are higher when filled with helium, so the pitch of the person's voice will be higher (the traveling waves in helium, thus, do not take as long to bounce back and forth in these cavities).

The vibration of the helium in the vocal cavities acts as a source for the sound waves in the air between speaker and listener. These waves in the air have the same (high) frequency as the standing waves in the vocal cavities.

7.   Pressure is the perpendicular force per unit area. Since the eardrum has about 20 times the area of the oval window, the pressure on the oval window would be 20 times that experienced by the eardrum if the same force were transmitted. In fact, the text points out that the force is actually mechanically doubled by the bones linking the two membranes, and so the pressure at the oval window is actually about 40 times that at the eardrum.

8.   Catgut strings are wrapped with fine wire to increase their mass, which for a given tension reduces the speed of wave propagation in the string and, therefore, lowers its fundamental frequency. In contrast, since the wavelength is fixed by the length of the string it does not change.

9.   Just as tube lengths may be chosen to resonate at certain frequencies by having constructively interfering standing waves, other lengths can be chosen to produce destructive interference.

10.   Warm air is less dense than cool air, so the speed of sound is greater in warm air. Since the wavelength is determined by the length of the organ pipe (whose temperature dependence can be neglected here), the fundamental frequency (which determines the pitch) will increase with increasing room temperature and decrease with falling temperature.

11.   The smaller the vibrating area supporting the sound wave, the less acoustic energy it will radiate. Acoustic isolation decouples the vibrating masses from the environment (walls, floors) and minimizes propagation of the vibrations into solid materials beyond the actual machine, preventing walls and floor from acting as a sounding board.

Making surfaces thicker reduces the amplitude of vibrations and helps damp them, thus, reducing the noise level.

12.   Frets indicate where fingers should be placed to produce successive notes. The length of the vibrating string is determined by the distance between the finger and the bridge. The relationship between frequency intervals and the corresponding wavelength changes (string length changes) is not linear and the length changes become smaller at higher frequencies.

The pitch is determined by the frequency of the fundamental $f = v/2L$, where L is the length of the string. Consider two successive notes in the musical scale with frequencies f_1 and f_2 ($f_2 > f_1$). As a result, their lengths are in the same ratio as their frequencies, $L_1/L_2 = f_2/f_1$, and if $L_1 = L_2 + \Delta L$, then $1 + \Delta L/L_2 = f_2/f_1$, or $\Delta L = (f_2/f_1 - 1)L_2$. For any two successive notes in the equally tempered scale of Table 12-3, f_2/f_1 is constant (indeed, $f_2/f_1 = 2^{1/12} = 1.0595$). Therefore, the distance ΔL between frets is proportional to L, so as f increases, L and ΔL decrease.

13.   Standing waves: Nodes and antinodes appear at different points in space, but they are present at all times. In order for standing waves to be produced, the superposing waves must have the same frequency. Furthermore, this frequency must be one of the natural frequencies of the system.

Beats: Maxima and minima in intensity occur at the same point in space, but at different times. In order for beats to be produced, the superposing waves must have different frequencies. However, the frequencies must not differ by much if the beats are to be noticeable.

14.   First consider the connection between frequency and wavelength: $c = f\lambda$, so $\lambda = c/f$. Decreasing the frequency of the sound wave increases its wavelength. The wavelength sets the scale of the drawing and of the sound waves the drawing represents. Increasing λ, therefore, increases all distances, in particular, the distance between C and D.

15.   The noise present is a sound wave. With real-time sampling techniques, the amplitude of the noise in the audible range of frequencies is found, and a speaker generates a wave with opposite phase. The sum of a sound crest and a sound trough is zero. The additional noise is such that the addition of the "anti-noise" gives a wave of near zero amplitude. The result is nearly silence.

16.   If the motion is truly at right angles to the line of sight from the listener to the source, there will be no velocity component towards or away from the listener and hence, no Doppler effect . This is also true at the instant when a source moving by a person in a straight line is at right angles to the line of sight, but before and after this instant, there will be a Doppler effect.

17.   The Doppler effect gives the greatest frequency difference when the observer is moving the fastest towards or away from the source. From what we know, the greatest speed for the swinging child occurs at the bottom of the trajectory (point C). Thus, point C will allow the child to experience both the highest frequency compared to the whistle's normal frequency (as the child moves toward the whistle) and the lowest frequency compared to the whistle's normal frequency (as the child moves away from the whistle).

18.   If a wind is blowing and the observer is at rest with respect to the source, the observer will not notice a Doppler shift and the frequency will not be altered. This situation is completely equivalent to the air being still, the source moving at the wind speed away from (toward) the observer and the observer moving at the same speed toward (away from) the source. The effects at source and observer cancel one another out completely, since the wavelength change at the source is compensated for by the changed speed with which the observer intercepts the waves.

19.   Both a sonic boom and an explosion produce shock waves by having the source of the sound waves moving faster than the speed of sound in the medium. In one case it is the aircraft, in the other it is the exploding object.

Chapter 13

1. For equal masses of iron and aluminum, the aluminum will have more atoms because the mass of an aluminum atom is less than the mass of an iron atom.

2. The linear coefficient of expansion (as in a bimetallic strip), the volume coefficient of expansion, and the electrical resistance may all be used for temperature sensing.

3. It takes 100 °C to get from freezing water to boiling water (at sea level), while it takes 180 °F to go from freezing to boiling. Therefore, the Celsius degree is a larger temperature interval than the Fahrenheit degree.

4. Since body temperature is 37 °C, 40 °C is a fever! To translate, 1 Fahrenheit degree is $\frac{5}{9}$ the size of a Celsius degree, and conversely, 1 Celsius degree is $\frac{9}{5}$ the size of a Fahrenheit degree. Also, the Fahrenheit scale for freezing is 32 °F, while the Celsius scale for freezing is 0 °C. Thus, $T(°F) = \frac{9}{5} T(°C) + 32$, giving a Fahrenheit temperature of $\frac{9}{5}$ (40) + 32 = 72 + 32 = 104.

5. The lower strip has a greater coefficient of linear expansion than the upper one, so when the temperature rises, the bimetallic strip will bend upward, away from contact, and will shut off the heater. When the temperature drops, the lower strip will contract more, causing the bimetallic strip to bend down and make contact, turning on the heater.

6. Aluminum has a larger coefficient of expansion than iron, so the aluminum will be on the outside of the curve when the bimetallic strip is heated.

7. The parameter L_0 should be the initial length. Under certain conditions, it does matter which length is used. (Using differential thermal expansions to make tight fits, for example.)

8. The "U" sections act like springs when the pipes expand or contract and keep them from breaking.

9. No. The expansion relation is $\Delta L = L_0 \alpha \Delta T$; therefore, the unit of length enters on both sides of the equal sign. This relation holds for any measurement units for distance, as long as they are the same on both sides.

10. Since the coefficient of volume expansion of mercury is greater than that of lead, the density of the mercury will decrease more than that of the lead and relatively more of it will have to be displaced to support the weight of the lead. Therefore, the lead will float lower as the temperature is raised.

11. If the water is added rapidly, it will produce rapid local cooling and the sudden contraction may cause fractures. If the engine is not running, the water pump will not operate and the water will stay in one place and possibly cause harm, whereas if the engine is running, the pump will distribute the water throughout the whole cooling system.

12. The local expansion or contraction of the glass may set up stresses larger than can be supported by the glass.

13.   Because it is first exposed to a differing temperature, the glass expands first, enlarging the mercury reservoir and causing the mercury column to descend before the glass has had a chance to conduct the thermal energy to the mercury, so it can then expand.

14.   Because of the smaller expansion coefficient of Pyrex, the stresses in Pyrex are smaller, and therefore, Pyrex can take a greater thermal shock without breaking.

15.   The relation between the period of a pendulum and the pendulum length, L, is $T = 2\pi(L/g)^{1/2}$. On a hot day, L will be longer, so T will be greater (so the frequency will be lower). The clock, therefore, runs slower at 30 °C than on a day with a temperature of 20 °C.

16.   Water is anomalous in that it does not expand uniformly with temperature. Above 4 °C, it expands when the temperature increases; below 4 °C, it also expands as the temperature decreases. Water expands even more when it freezes (this is the origin of the warning that you see only 10% of an iceberg; 90% is hidden below water). The can is designed for a small amount of expansion, not a 10% expansion in volume. When it freezes, the expansion increases the can's volume by deforming the can's surface. The can's surface will expand where it is easiest (where the can is weakest). This will generally be near the bends, but mechanical problems with flattening the aluminum sheet of which the can is made can lead to seemingly random parts of the can expanding.

17.   The ideal gas laws are an approximation that assumes the atoms or molecules are dimensionless, non-interacting points, and therefore, their actual size does not enter into the equations. At STP, the average separation between the gas molecules is much, much greater than the size of a molecule, so the approximation is a good one.

18.   When the piston compresses the gas, the molecules gain momentum as they rebound from the piston that is doing work on them, and they gain kinetic energy, causing the temperature of the gas to increase. When the gas expands against a piston it does work on the piston, the molecules lose momentum rebounding from the piston, suffer a decrease in kinetic energy, and the temperature decreases.

19.   Charles's Law states that the volume of a gas is proportional to its absolute temperature if the pressure is constant. Since the kinetic energy increases with absolute temperature and since the pressure results from the force the rebounding molecules exert on the walls, the only way to keep the pressure constant as the temperature is increased is to increase the area of the walls, i.e., the volume. If the temperature is decreased, so is the kinetic energy, and we need to reduce the wall area, and hence the volume, to keep the pressure constant.

20.   Gay-Lussac's Law states that at constant volume, the pressure is directly proportional to the absolute temperature. Since the average kinetic energy is proportional to the absolute temperature, and the pressure is proportional to kinetic energy (because of the average force exerted by the molecules on the walls due to their rebound), the pressure will be proportional to the absolute temperature.

21.   At a given temperature, the average translational kinetic energies of both oxygen and nitrogen are equal; since nitrogen has the smaller mass, the average speed of the nitrogen molecules will be greater than that of the oxygen molecules. The maximum altitude h reachable by a molecule with initial speed v ($h = v^2/2g$) and the escape speed from

21., continued

Earth's gravity are both independent of mass, so more of the nitrogen molecules will have speeds that allow them to get to very high altitudes, and the nitrogen/oxygen ratio will increase with height to a maximum at the outer fringes of the atmosphere.

22.   Almost all the molecules of the Moon's atmosphere have already escaped into space over geological time scales.

23.   The Maxwell distribution of speeds is not symmetrical because the lowest speed is zero, while there is no cutoff on the high side.

24.   The "hotter" molecules have more kinetic energy and, thus, tend to move toward the cold side, moving the particles with them. On the cold side, the molecules lose kinetic energy and slow down, and the much more massive particles come to rest there. Another way of looking at this is that there is a "wind" blowing from the hot to the cold side that moves the particles to the cold side.

25.   The attractive force between the molecules of alcohol must be weaker than that between the molecules of water.

26.   The evaporation of perspiration is inhibited by humid air, reducing the effect of evaporative cooling on the skin. The net rate of evaporation on a humid day is reduced because the number of water-vapor molecules condensing on the skin is greater.

27.   Yes. If the pressure is reduced below the vapor pressure of water at 20 °C (about 1/10 of atmospheric pressure), the water will boil at that temperature.

Chapter 14

1.   It goes into heating the orange juice by increasing the average KE of the molecules.

2.   a) Temperature does not flow—heat does.
        b) The temperature changes are not generally equal. However, under certain circumstances, depending on the initial temperatures, masses, and heat capacities involved, the magnitude of the temperature changes may be equal.

3.   a) No, it will flow from the object at the higher temperature to the object at the lower temperature. This may or may not be the same as a flow from the object at higher internal energy, depending on the masses and heat capacities of the objects.
        b) Yes, as discussed in (a) above. It is temperature differences that lead to a flow of thermal energy. Even if the internal energies are the same, there may be different temperatures for the two objects, and it is temperature differences that determine the flow.

4.   When the water freezes, it gives off the heat of fusion, increasing the temperature of the surrounding air, which may save the plant. (The latent heat of fusion of water is very large.) During the freezing process the temperature of the water in contact with the plant does not go below freezing, causing the water to act as an insulator.

5.   A given mass of water is able to transfer a larger amount of thermal energy at a given temperature than a material having a smaller specific heat.

6.   The water evaporating from the canteen jacket absorbs its heat of vaporization from the canteen and helps cool the canteen and its contents.

7.   The condensing steam transfers its heat of vaporization to the skin.

8.   The latent heat of vaporization necessary for evaporation comes from the water and reduces its internal energy, thereby reducing its temperature. From the molecular standpoint, it is the most energetic molecules that evaporate, leaving behind those having a lower average kinetic energy.

9.   No. As long as the water is boiling, it remains at the same temperature (its boiling point at the given pressure; that is, 100 °C at normal atmospheric pressure).

10.   No. In fact, it heats the air slightly from the friction of the blades and because the motor gets hot.. It is used to create an artificial wind to replace hot and humid air and facilitate the evaporation of perspiration, a process which removes heat from our bodies and makes us feel cooler.

11.   Recall that temperature is defined as the average translational kinetic energy of the gas molecules. High in Earth's atmosphere there are fewer gas molecules, but those that are present have higher average translational kinetic energy than those near the ground, and therefore, have a higher temperature. However, since the density of the atmosphere is so low up there, the thermal energy per unit volume is very small, and little heat would be transferred to an animal.

12.   Snow has wonderful insulating properties (its thermal conductivity is low). Eskimos once used snow for housing because of this property. Ice has a relatively low thermal conductivity on its own, but snow contains air, which has a very low thermal conductivity indeed (it is one hundred times smaller than that of ice).

13.   Water has a greater thermal conductivity and a greater specific heat than sand. Water has to absorb a lot more energy to get hot than sand does (this is the primary reason it feels cooler), and it conducts thermal energy away faster.

14.   Air has a very low thermal conductivity. Even air trapped between the thin layers of newspaper and between the newspapers and the person acts as a good thermal insulator. Therefore, a person's internally-generated body heat can warm nearby pockets of air and the still air will keep the vicinity relatively warm. Even on cold nights, thin sheets of paper can keep a person comfortable.

As you may recall, however, the rate of heat transfer to the environment depends on the temperature difference; if the outside air is cold enough, this transfer rate can exceed the rate at which a person is able to generate heat through metabolic processes, and the person may freeze to death.

15.   Without a return vent ,the normal circulation pattern would be disturbed. Normally, the heated air enters a room at floor level, rises to the ceiling, and, as it cools, sinks back to the floor, where it enters the air return, goes down to the furnace, is reheated, and repeats the cycle. If the air return is blocked, the cool air interferes with the warm air, the smooth circulation is disrupted, and the heating process becomes very inefficient.

16.   In winter, the warm air near the ceiling should be moved (as far as possible without an uncomfortable draft) to nearer the floor to increase comfort. In summer, a cooling breeze is welcome because it can enhance the rate of evaporation from the skin. Thus, in summer, the fan should be set to drive air downward from the ceiling (left picture below), which will make a large concentrated descending column of air that will pass by people underneath. In winter (right below), it should be set to pull air upward from the floor; this air is still warm and is spread out over a wider volume, forcing the warmer air near the ceiling to move toward the floor around the periphery of the room while avoiding a direct draft on people.

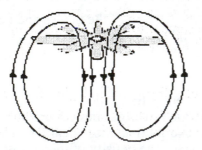 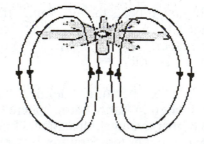

Summer arrangement   Winter arrangement

17.   The heat transferred by conduction through a substance depends not only on the temperature difference, the thermal conductivity, and the cross-sectional area, but also inversely on the thickness. So the greater the thickness of the garment, the less thermal energy it will conduct away from your body, and the warmer you will be. As one can see from Table 14-4, the air trapped between the fluffed-up down has a slightly lower thermal conductivity than the down itself.

18.   The fins have a fairly large surface area, from which thermal energy may be transferred to the environment. The alternative would be a

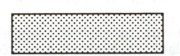

a)

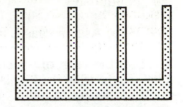

b)

solid piece of similar volume but smaller surface area. Since the rate of heat transfer (of any kind) depends on the surface area, the larger area will radiate the greatest amount of thermal energy per time. The objects in (a) and (b) have equal volumes, but (b) has a much larger surface area.

19.   As the air over the land is heated, it rises and is replaced by relatively cooler air from above the water, causing a sea breeze.

20.   The concrete slab has a large heat capacity, and being in contact with the ground, tends to maintain the ground temperature. By contrast, if the air can freely circulate under the house, convection and radiation are able to transfer heat away from the house and cool it.

21.   In the absence of clouds, Earth can radiate heat directly into space.

22.   a) The silvering (see the picture to the right) reduces heat loss by radiation, since silver reflects the radiation coming both from the outside (and keeps it out) and the inside (and keeps it in).

   b) The vacuum reduces heat loss by conduction.

23.   If you put the thermometer into the direct sunlight rather than the shade, you could be measuring the temperature of the thermometer as it heats up from the solar radiation, instead of the ambient air temperature.

24.   The thermal energy produced by a warm-blooded animal is proportional to its volume, while the heat loss is proportional to its surface area. In a tiny premature baby, the surface to volume ratio can be very large. At the same time, its heat generating and stabilization system may not yet be fully developed. These factors could cause the baby's temperature to drop to dangerously low levels.

25.   Heat sources for a house: We will compute all sources in kWh. If joules are desired, note that 1 kWh = 3.6 x 10^6 J. Domestic heating gas is billed in units of CCF (1 CCF = 100 cubic feet) and 1 cubic foot of gas produces 1000 Btu of energy (1 Btu = 1055 J).

   a) At 40° latitude, assume a roof area of 120 m^2, e = 0.5, and cloud cover half the time; and use $\Delta Q/\Delta t$ = (1000 W/m^2) e A cos 40° for clear sky and (400 W/m^2) e A cos 40° for cloudy sky. With these assumptions, we get $\Delta Q/\Delta t$ = 32 kW, so the energy captured per day (assuming 12 daylight hours on average) is 32 kW x 12 h = 384 kWh.

Chapter 14

25., continued

b) Assume gas is used for heating house and water. Monthly gas consumption for the water heater is determined from gas bills during summer months. We find 1545 CCF total for the year, of which 200 CCF is for the water heater (12 months), leaving 1345 CCF for heating the house (6 months). Computing the average power in kW and multiplying by 24 hours, we find during the heating season, 209 kWh per day for the house and year-round 16 kWh per day for the water heater.

c) Cooking stove, microwave, toaster, iron: 1000 W each when operating. Assume each is used half an hour per day on average. This adds 2 kWh.

d) Refrigerator: Assume a 550 W compressor and a 25% duty cycle; this gives 0.550 kW x 6 h = 3.3 kWh. This is the energy to run the compressor and most of it goes into heating the environment. If the coefficient of performance (CP) of a refrigerator is 3, an additional 9.9 kWh of thermal energy per day is pumped out of the refrigerator into the kitchen. Although the latter does not add to the overall thermal energy of the house, it does raise the temperature of the kitchen.

e) Radios, stereos, TV, computers, etc., total 1000 W x 5 h = 5 kWh.

f) Lighting gives 500 W x 8 h = 4 kWh.

g) Heat transferred from people at 100 W each every 24 h, or 2.4 kWh per person per day.

26.   a) 1. Convection   2. Conduction   3. Conduction and radiation

b) Heavy curtains reduce convection, radiation, and conduction. The former acts by providing a physical barrier to moving air, the second acts by being more opaque to radiation than transparent glass. The curtain reduces conduction because the air trapped within the thick drapery material has a lower thermal conductivity than the glass. The curtain also separates the cool air layer on the window side from the warm air in the room, thus, lowering the temperature gradient between the two sides of the glass, and therefore, reducing conduction.

27.   The wood is a much poorer thermal conductor than the metal, so the rate of heat transfer of the wood to your skin when you pick it up is much lower for the wood.

28.   In Case (a), the cold milk is added just after the coffee is poured, and then the mixture cools by conduction for 3 minutes. In Case (b), the coffee cools by conduction for 3 minutes, and then the cold milk is added. Which case has the lower temperature 3 minutes after the coffee is poured?

We assume that adding cold milk drops the temperature instantaneously and that the milk and the coffee have the same specific heat. In adding the milk, the thermal energy lost by the coffee is equal to the thermal energy gained by the milk. Immediately after the milk is added, the temperature of the mixture

$$T_{mix} = \frac{MT_c + mT_m}{M+m},$$ (1)

28., continued

where T_c and T_m are the temperatures of the coffee and the milk, respectively, before they are combined, M is the mass of coffee and m is the mass of the milk.

According to the Giancoli text, the rate of heat flow by conduction is
$$\Delta Q/\Delta t = k\, A\, (T - T_{env})/L,$$
where T_{env} is the temperature of the environment and T is the temperature of the liquid in the cup. Over a short time interval Δt, the loss of heat by the liquid is
$$\Delta Q = k\, A\, (T - T_{env})\, \Delta t/L = M_{total}\, c\, \Delta T, \tag{2}$$
where ΔT is the decrease in the temperature of the liquid as a result of conduction, M_{total} is the mass of the liquid, and c is the specific heat of the liquid. Unless one uses calculus, one can apply this equation only to situations where ΔT is small compared to T; we therefore assume $\Delta T \ll T$ in the time interval of interest. The answer then is that most of the cooling is provided by adding the milk, so it does not much matter whether you add the milk at the beginning or 3 minutes later. In Case (b), the cooling by conduction is greater than in Case (a) because the temperature difference between the liquid and the environment is greater and the mass being cooled is smaller, so Case (b) will have a slightly lower temperature.

The following example illustrates the situation. Suppose that the coffee has a temperature $T_c = 95.0\ °C$ when first poured, the milk has a temperature $T_m = 5.0\ °C$, the mixture is 10% milk, and the temperature of the environment is 22.0 °C. In Case (a), equation (1) gives $T_{mix} = 86.0\ °C$ just after the milk is added. The liquid with mass
$$M_{a\ total} = M + m = 1.1\,M$$
then cools by conduction from 86 °C by an amount $(\Delta T)_a$. In Case (b), the liquid with mass $M_{b\ total} = M$ cools by conduction for 3 minutes from 95 °C by an amount $(\Delta T)_b$. Since the values of k, A, L, and c are the same in both cases, we have from equation (2)
$$(\Delta T)_b/(\Delta T)_a = \frac{(T - T_{env})_b}{(T - T_{env})_a}\,\frac{M_{a\ total}}{M_{b\ total}} = \frac{(95°C - 22°C)}{(86°C - 22°C)}\,\frac{1.1\,M}{M} = 1.25.$$

This assumes that ΔT is small compared to T. In Case (a), the final temperature is
$$T_{a,f} = 86.0\ °C - (\Delta T)_a.$$
In Case (b), the coffee at $T_b = 95\ °C - 1.25\,(\Delta T)_a$ is then mixed with the milk at 5.0 °C, to give a final temperature [from equation (1)] of
$$T_{b,f} = 0.5\ °C + 0.9\,[95\ °C - 1.25\,(\Delta T)_a] = 86.0\ °C - 1.13\,(\Delta T)_a,$$
which is cooler than Case (a) but not by much, since $(\Delta T)_a$ is assumed to be only a few degrees. Proper treatment of the situation when $(\Delta T)_a$ is more than a few degrees is beyond the level of this text (see T. Greenslade, *Phys. Teach.* **32**, 145 (1994) for experiments and a discussion of the more general case).

Chapter 15

1.   Some of the internal energy (equal to the heat of vaporization) is emitted to the environment. Heat is exchanged, but no work is done.

2.   When the gas is compressed, work is done *on* it and W is negative. ΔU increases and since U is proportional to T, so does the temperature. When the gas expands, *it* does work, W is positive and ΔU is negative and T decreases. (We assume no heat transfer and so Q = 0.)

3.   Since Q - W = 0 here, if W = 3700 J, then Q = 3700 J.

4.   Since the work is the area under the curve on the P vs. V diagram, more work is done in the isothermal process AB than in process ADB.

5.   Yes. This is true of every isothermal process. See Questions 3 and 4 above.

6.   Same as Question 2.

7.   Mechanical energy can be completely transformed into internal energy. As an example, consider a stone falling to the ground and coming to rest. Its mechanical energy is completely transformed to internal energy, increasing the temperature of the stone and the ground.

Heat cannot be completely transformed into mechanical energy because this would violate the Second Law.

8.   No. A household refrigerator pumps thermal energy from its inside into the room and therefore, the room cannot be cooled that way. However, if the refrigerator door is left open and you stand in front of it, you will be cooler, while the air behind the refrigerator will be warmer. On balance, no heat is removed from the room. In fact, it will be increased by the heat transferred from operation of the compressor motor.

9.   No. W/Q would not be a useful definition of efficiency of a heat engine because efficiency should be a measure of the ratio of work done to energy input and should never exceed unity, which W/Q can do.

10.   a) Internal combustion engine: T_H is the temperature of the exploding mixture; T_L is the temperature of the air at exhaust.
       b) Steam engine: T_H is the temperature of the steam in boiler; T_L is the temperature of the condenser.

11.   A 10 °C decrease in T_L gives greater improvement than 10 °C increase in T_H. This follows from the algebraic expression for the efficiency, $\varepsilon = \dfrac{T_H - T_L}{T_H} = 1 - \dfrac{T_L}{T_H}$.

Let us subtract Δ from T_L in the above expression in one case, obtaining
$$\varepsilon = \frac{T_H - T_L + \Delta}{T_H}$$
and add Δ to T_H in the other, giving
$$\varepsilon = \frac{T_H - T_L + \Delta}{T_H + \Delta}.$$

11., continued

Taking the ratio of the two resulting expressions and expanding, the ratio is $\dfrac{T_H + \Delta}{T_H}$, we see that, for $T_H > T_L$, the ratio is greater than one. This shows that decreasing T_L by a given amount increases the efficiency more than increasing T_H by the same amount.

12.   In any small local area, to extract energy from the ocean, there would have to be a heat engine that took ocean water at the ocean temperature and exhausted the water, also at the (same) ocean temperature. Any such process would violate the Second Law unless one had access to a lower temperature reservoir than the ocean; and in the local area, there is no such reservoir.

On a larger scale, one could in principle exploit the temperature differences between warm surface waters and cooler waters in the ocean abysses, or those differences between equatorial and polar seas. At present, the engineering problems and costs involved make such an enterprise impractical.

13.   a) Adiabatic gas expansion: Entropy stays the same (no heat transfer).

b) Isothermal gas expansion: Entropy increases (heat must be added).

14.   a) Green leaves turning color in autumn and falling to the ground.

b) A tornado touching down and destroying houses.

c) An abandoned car left outdoors slowly rusting away.

It is *EXTREMELY* unlikely that the reverse process would occur of its own accord.

15.   The liquid iron has more entropy than the solid because it has less order than the crystalline solid iron. (The kinetic energy of random molecular motion is higher in the liquid.)

16.   The gas diffuses out of the bottle until it fills the room. The reverse process is so improbable that, for practical purposes, we consider it impossible. It would require a spontaneous negative entropy change.

Other examples include a drop of ink falling into a glass of water and coloring the water, cream mixing with black coffee, or an ordered deck of cards being honestly shuffled. Although the latter has only 52 elements instead of the typically 10^{23} atoms in the former examples, the likelihood of getting back to the original ordering is still vanishingly small.

17.   If all the air molecules in front of your face were spontaneously just to happen to move away elsewhere, leaving you gasping, the First Law would have been obeyed but the Second Law would have been violated.

Chapter 15

17., continued

As another example, suppose you filled a large cooking pot with water, put it on your electric stove, and turned on the heating element. If the heating element got very hot and the water froze, the First Law would be obeyed, because in addition to the electricity heating the element, some of the internal energy of the water as well as the heat of fusion when it turns into ice is added to the element, thus, conserving energy. However, the Second Law would be violated.

18.   No. You and your environment have now become the system and that larger system's entropy is increasing overall as you do work to make your papers neater, even though some regions of the system may show entropy decreases.

19.   "You can't get something for nothing" would be a statement of the conservation of energy: $\Delta U = Q - W$. "You can't even break even": $S = 0$ would be breaking even, but it must be true that $S > 0$ for any real process. Fig. 15-13 shows what breaking even would imply.

20.   a) Friction degrades mechanical energy into thermal energy.

b) A waterfall degrades gravitational potential energy into internal energy.

c) Lightning degrades electrical potential energy into internal energy.

21.   a) Smashed up cars at an intersection would be magically restored and would drive away backwards from the intersection.

b) A red wine stain on a white dress would shrink, disappear, and then wine would jump back into the glass.

c) In a western shoot-out, the bloodied and presumably dead loser would get up from the ground unbloodied, and aim his gun at the winner (and maybe even get off a shot).

d) Objects that do not normally float upwards from the ground would do this with disconcerting frequency.

22.   No. The Second Law is relevant for *closed* systems. The system composed of the organisms is *open*, not closed, because energy is received from the environment external to the system. This outside energy can allow the *local* decrease in entropy. Of course, in the entire system (including the source of energy), entropy is increased in the process of generating the energy more than it has been decreased locally. Thus, overall, entropy for the closed system has increased.

1.   Charge a glass rod by rubbing it with a cloth. The glass rod then has a positive charge. See if the comb is attracted or repelled by the charged comb. If the former, the comb is negative; if the latter, it is positive. In practice, because the electric forces are on the order of millinewtons, it may be easier to charge a suspended pith ball with the glass rod and see whether the pith ball is attracted to, or repelled by, the comb.

2.   A shirt clings because it has acquired a net charge by rubbing against other clothes in the dryer. Dry air reduces the loss of charge by leaking off.

3.   The polar water molecules are attracted to the charged particles.

4.   Molecules in neutral paper become polarized in the presence of a positively charged rod. (The negative end of molecule is closest to positive rod.)

rod   polarized molecules

5.   The charged ruler induces an opposite charge on the paper (see Figure in answer to Question 4). This causes the paper to be attracted to the ruler. On a humid day, charge will leak off quickly from the ruler because the excess charge is attracted to the polar water-vapor molecules in the air.

Note: The text of the book explains why uncharged metals are attracted to a charged rod, but fails to do this for uncharged insulators. The only mention is in the caption to the color photograph of the comb picking up pieces of paper (p. 476), where induced "separation of charge" is mentioned. This is ambiguous and the student will tend to associate it with the metal rod in Fig. 16-7, where the same phrase occurs.

6.   The net charge, in terms of the unit charge, is the difference between the total number of protons and electrons in the conductor. The free charges are the conduction electrons, which are free to move in the conductor because they are not bound to any particular atom. Note that a conductor with a net charge of zero still contains "free charges."

7.   Because the others are bound to atoms and not free to move in the metal.

8.   As leaves separate, the ends of the leaves rise. The force of gravity exerted by Earth keeps leaves from rising farther and thus, balances the electrical repulsion.

9.   In universal gravitation, masses always attract. In Coulomb's Law, unlike charges attract and like charges repel. There is only one kind of mass, but there are two kinds of charge. Also, electric force is much stronger than gravitational. (Compute the Coulomb force and gravitational force between the electron and proton in the hydrogen atom and compare.)

10.   a) The gravitational force is very weak and ordinarily not noticeable unless at least one of the masses involved is an astronomical object, such as the earth. It requires a very sensitive Cavendish experiment to demonstrate the gravitational force between ordinary objects.

       b) The electrical force is much stronger than the gravitational force, but because of the fact that positive and negative charges usually cancel completely, we are not aware of it most of the time. However, the slightest imbalance of charge will cause "static cling" of our clothes, or sparks to fly from our fingers to a metal door knob if we have been walking across a certain type of rug (e.g., one made of synthetic fiber) on a dry day.

11.   The electric force is conservative because the work done in moving a charge from point A to point B is independent of path. Notice that Coulomb's law is very similar in form to Newton's Law of Universal Gravitation, and the examples in Chapter 6 showed that the work done against the gravitational force in moving an object between points A and B is independent of path. (This question more properly belongs at the end of the next chapter, in which electric potential is introduced.)

12.   If the numerator in Coulomb's Law contained the sum of the charges rather than their product, two equal and opposite charges would not attract each other as observed, since the expression would vanish.

13.   Touching the ruler may transfer some of the charge on the ruler to the paper, giving both charge of equal sign and causing repulsion.

14.   Since the test charge itself produces a field, we want to make it as small as possible to minimize perturbing the field we are trying to measure.

15.   Since by convention the direction of $\vec{E}$ is the direction of the force on a positive charge, we can use a negative test charge, so long as we remember that in this case the direction of $\vec{E}$ is opposite to direction of force on charge.

16.   Reverse arrows on field lines of Fig. 16-29 (b) on p. 491.

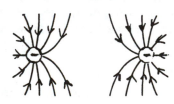

17.   The field is strongest on the right, weakest on the left. Recall that, the stronger the electric field, the closer together the electric field lines are.

18.   The electric field is strongest at A, weaker at B (since there is a greater separation between field lines there), and zero at C. No vector is drawn at C because the force on a test charge there is zero. At A and B, the direction of the force is drawn tangentially to the field line that would go through that point.

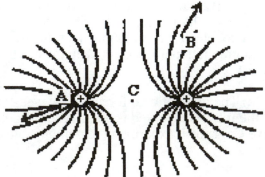

Chapter 16

19.   Lines of force cannot cross because they are defined to show the direction of the electric force on a positive charge at a given point in space. At a crossing point, this direction would not be defined.

20.   Force, and hence acceleration point along the field direction, which is tangential to the field line as shown by the straight arrow in the figure. The direction of the velocity depends also on the initial velocity of the test charge and will generally not be along any field line.

21.   To determine qualitatively what happens, imagine the test charge as large as the charge on the sphere. The field outside the unperturbed sphere is the same as that due to an equivalent point charge at the center of the sphere. Since both charges have the same sign, the field due to both will look like Fig. 16-29 (b), showing that the presence of the test charge reduces the field and F/q will be less than the undisturbed field. If q is made arbitrarily small, F will become small and the ratio F/q will be defined as the field strength at that point. Otherwise, the field at the position of a point charge, no matter how small, would be undefined.

Another way to determine the effect of the test charge in this particular case involving a charged conducting sphere is to make use of the fact that the positive test charge will attract negative charges as the test charge approaches the conducting sphere, and that these negative charges will weaken the field that existed before the test charge approached.

Chapter 17

1.   a) Yes.

b) Not necessarily. A force may be exerted to do positive work on the charge for part of the path, and an equal amount of negative work on the charge for the rest of the path. In that case, the work done against the field and by the field will add to zero.

2.   No. If equipotentials crossed, there would be two different potentials at the crossing point, and hence, that point could not lie on an equipotential line or surface. Because equipotentials are always perpendicular to lines of force (fields), they cannot cross since lines of force do not cross. (See Question 19 in Chapter 16, which asks why lines of force cannot cross.)

3.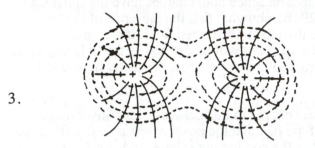

4.   a) The resultant field will vanish at the midpoint, since the two field vectors add to zero there.

b) We assume here that the potential is taken to be zero at an infinite distance from all charges. The potential is a scalar and since both potentials are positive, their sum is nonzero at any finite distance from the charges.

5.   Twice as great, because $q \Delta V = \Delta(\frac{1}{2} mv^2)$. (A 400 electronvolt electron may still be treated classically. At much higher energies, relativistic kinematics must be used instead.)

6.   A negative charge will move toward a region of higher potential, whereas a positive charge will move toward a region of lower potential. In both cases the potential energy will decrease. Since $\Delta PE = Q \Delta V$, for negative Q, we have (-)(+) = (-) while for positive Q, we have (+)(-) = (-).

7.   a) The electric potential at a point is electric potential energy per unit charge. The electric field at a point is electric force per unit charge.

b) Since the electric potential is potential energy per unit charge, the electric potential energy of a charge must equal the charge times the electric potential. (Recall that reference potential is arbitrary and only potential differences are meaningful.)

8.   No. Consider the dipole in Fig. 16-29 (a). The potential at the midpoint of the line joining the charges is zero. The field is not.

9.   If potential is constant, the electric field $\overrightarrow{E} = 0$, since $E = \Delta V/d = 0$.

10.   a) The gravitational field changes inversely as distance squared ($\propto \frac{1}{r^2}$) for r > R, where R is radius of Earth.

        b) In same region, gravitational potential changes inversely as r ($\propto \frac{1}{r}$) .

11.   Yes. This will be true for a negatively charged particle, which has its greatest potential energy at the lowest electric potential. Such a particle will "fall" to a higher potential, and thus, decrease its potential energy. The change in electric potential is defined as $\Delta V = \Delta PE/q$, so if $\Delta PE < 0$ and $q < 0$, then $\Delta V > 0$.

12.   a) V would be 10 volts lower at other points.
        b) E would remain the same everywhere, since it depends only on the voltage DIFFERENCE between points.

13.   The two plates acquire equal and opposite charges because any imbalance would be quickly eliminated. Suppose the positive plate had a slightly greater charge than the negative. Electrons from the negative battery terminal would be attracted towards the positive plate, but could not get across the space between the plates. Therefore, it would increase the charge on the negative plate until the net charge on the two plates was zero. A similar thing would happen if the negative plate had excess charge. This will be true even if the two plates are of different sizes and shapes.

14.   It means that while C depends on the geometry, it does not depend on Q or V, and in fact, is the proportionality constant relating the two: $Q = C V$.

15.   Energy stored = $U = \frac{1}{2} QV = \frac{1}{2} CV^2$.
        a) Q fixed
        $V = V_0/K$, where K is the dielectric constant
        $U = \frac{1}{2} QV = \frac{1}{2} QV_0/K = U_0/K$, which decreases, since K>1
        b) V fixed
        $C = KC_0$
        $U = \frac{1}{2} CV^2 = KU_0$, which increases (energy is supplied by battery)

Chapter 18

1.   The total charge the battery can supply before it runs down is measured in ampere-hours. Since an ampere is one coulomb per second, one ampere-hour is 3600 coulombs.

2.   Inside the cell, the chemical reaction between the dissimilar electrodes and the electrolyte causes electrons to flow from the positive to the negative terminal. In fact, this is how the terminals become positive and negative.

3.   The heart is the battery, blood is the charge, blood flow is the current, and the organs supplied with blood are circuit elements. The arteries are the wires from the battery to the elements and the veins the wires returning to the battery.

4.   Shown in off position. Moving either switch will turn on the light, after which either switch can turn it off again.

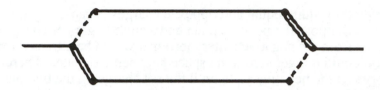

5.   Yes, there are several possibilities. Recall that $R = \rho \dfrac{L}{A}$, where A is the cross-sectional area and L is the length of the resistor. If the temperature is fixed, but the area may vary, we want to obtain $\rho_{Cu} \dfrac{L}{A_{Cu}} = \rho_{Al} \dfrac{L}{A_{Al}}$, so we take $\dfrac{A_{Al}}{A_{Cu}} = \dfrac{\rho_{Al}}{\rho_{Cu}}$. If D is the diameter of wire, then we require

$$\frac{\rho_{Al}}{\rho_{Cu}} = \frac{A_{Al}}{A_{Cu}} = \left(\frac{D_{Al}}{D_{Cu}}\right)^2 .$$

If the copper and aluminum wires are of the same area and length, it is possible to make them the same resistance if they are separately held at suitably different temperatures because of the temperature dependence of the resistivity.

Finally, it is possible in principle (assuming the linear temperature dependence of temperature on resistivity to persist indefinitely) to make the resistances equal when the copper and aluminum wires are of the same area and length at one certain temperature, by beginning at, say, room temperature and then requiring that $\rho_{Cu}(T) \dfrac{L}{A} = \rho_{Al}(T) \dfrac{L}{A}$, so that

$$\rho_{0\ Cu}(1 + \alpha_{Cu}\Delta T) = \rho_{0\ Al}(1 + \alpha_{Al}\Delta T),$$

or

$$\Delta T = \frac{\rho_{0\ Cu} - \rho_{0\ Al}}{(\rho_{0\ Cu})(\alpha_{Cu}) - (\rho_{0\ Al})(\alpha_{Al})} .$$

6.   a) Least R   b) Greatest R

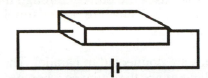

7.   In a car, there is so much mass of connected conducting material (engine, chassis, body) all at the same potential, that it can be used as a voltage reference and called ground. In fact, one of the battery terminals is "grounded" this way.

8.   There is no contradiction because V and I are not independent. The voltage across a resistor R, V, and the current through R, I, are related by Ohm's Law: $V = I R$. If this is substituted in $P = V^2/R$ we get $P = I^2 R$ and if $I = V/R$ is substituted in $P = I^2 R$, we get $P = V^2/R$.

9.   The filament breaks, opening the circuit and interrupting the current.

10.   When just turned on, the filament has a lower temperature, and thus, a lower resistance than after the light has been on for some time. Therefore, the rate of conversion of electrical energy into thermal energy, $P = V^2/R$, is greatest in the filament when the light is first turned on, so the filament is more likely to burn out then.

11.   V is constant here. Let $P_1 = 100$ W and $P_2 = 75$ W. Then, since $P = V^2/R$, $P_1/P_2 = R_2/R_1$. Thus, the 75 W bulb has higher resistance. Since $P = I V$, $I_1/I_2 = P_1/P_2$ and the 100 W bulb draws more current.

12.   Here we have to distinguish between the power transmitted and the power lost. The transmitted power is $P = I V$. Thus, the greater the voltage, the smaller the current and the smaller the $I^2 R$ loss for a given transmission line of resistance R. (Note: If we use V^2/R to calculate the power dissipated in the transmission line, V in this expression is the I R drop in the line, not the potential difference across the power source; the voltage drop in the line is reduced if I is reduced.)

13.   It is dangerous to replace a 15 A fuse that blows repeatedly with a 25 A fuse because whatever is blowing the 15 A fuse may not blow a 25 A fuse and could instead set the house on fire.

14.   The phenomenon called "persistence of vision" makes possible motion pictures and television, where successive images are displayed so rapidly that we do not notice any discontinuity. A frequency of 10 Hz corresponds to 1/10 of a second intervals; these are longer than the persistence of vision and begin to be noticed. Since the light output of electric lights fluctuates with the applied AC voltage, the lights begin to flicker at low enough frequencies.

15.   In (a), the batteries are connected in series. Compared to using only one of the batteries, this increases the potential difference across the bulb (by a factor of 2 for identical batteries) and so increases the current through the bulb (also by a factor of 2 for identical batteries), since $I = V/R$. Thus, the power supplied to the bulb, $P = IV$, will be greater (by a factor of 4 for identical batteries), and so the bulb will be brighter.

In (b) the batteries are connected in parallel. The potential difference across the bulb and the current in the filament are the same as when a single battery is used. Using two batteries provides a greater reservoir of charge and, therefore, will be able to provide current to the bulb for a longer time before going dead than a single battery.

16.   For any one instant of time when the current flowing through the filament is not zero, electrical energy is being converted to thermal energy at a rate $P = I^2 R$ as a result of collisions between the flowing charges and the atoms in the filament. This conversion of energy does not depend on the direction of current flow. Thus, the heated filament emits light independent of the direction of the current. At the instant when the current and the voltage reverse directions, the current in the filament is zero and no electrical energy is being converted to thermal energy (though the filament is still hot and will continue to glow for a while). At a frequency of 60 Hz (the Americas) or 50 Hz (Europe and Japan), this cooling occurs over too short a time interval to be noticeable due to persistence of vision.

17.   As the toaster is turned on, the current in the heating element increases from zero to a maximum value. Then, as the conductors increase in temperature, the resistance of the conductors increases. This means that the current $I = V/R$ decreases until a steady temperature is reached.

18.   No. The same current that enters a resistor leaves the resistor; otherwise charge would be accumulating on the resistor.

Chapter 19

1.   The bird can sit on a power line safely because its whole body is essentially at the same potential; actually, there may be a slight potential difference, but its legs are so close together that the potential difference between the feet is very small and, therefore, almost no charges flow (i.e., there is no current) through the bird. Leaning a metal ladder against the power line connects the voltage of the power line to ground, completing a circuit and causing charges to flow. If the resulting current goes through the body of the person retrieving the kite, it can produce electrocution.

2.   Christmas tree lights in series all go out if one bulb's filament breaks. Parallel Christmas tree bulbs will only turn off one light if the filament breaks.

3.   Yes, there are several ways to do this. If you connect 20 bulbs in series, you could put 120 V across the set and have only 6 V across each bulb. Also, if resistors were available, one might be able to connect them in series to get a set of terminals that have only 6 V across them. Finally, if one had both bulbs and resistors, it is possible that they could be arranged to give 6 V across the bulbs by connecting resistors in series with the bulbs.

4.   Brightness depends on the power transformed into thermal and radiant power in the bulb: $P = I^2R = V^2/R$. If the bulbs are in series, the higher resistance bulb has the greater voltage across it . Thus, if a bulb has a greater resistance, it will be brighter, since $P = IV = I^2R$ and the same current flows through both bulbs. So R_2 is brighter.

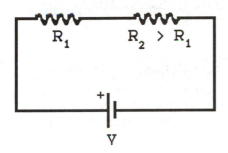

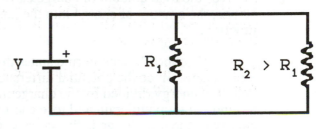

If the bulbs are connected in parallel, the voltage across each of the bulbs is the same, so a smaller current will flow through the bulb with greater resistance, since we may also write $P = V^2/R$. R_1 will be brighter, because it will carry a greater current.

5.   The emf is the "driving voltage" that sends electrons through wires in a circuit. It results from transformation of some other sort of energy into electrical energy. Such an emf will produce a potential difference in a circuit.

A potential difference is merely a difference in potential between two points that could come from any cause or combinations of causes, such as emfs, resistors, etc.

6.   The double outlets are connected in parallel because they can be used independently and each provides the full voltage. If they were in series, both outlets would have to be used to complete the circuit, and the voltage would be divided between the two loads.

6., continued

For example, if the outlets are in parallel and you connect a 100 W light bulb to the first outlet, you get 100 W of power. If you connect it to the other, you also get 100 W of power. Finally, if you connected 100 W bulbs to each outlet, each bulb would give 100 W. If the outlets were in series, each bulb would be dimmer than the individual bulb, drawing only 25 W. If you removed one bulb in the series configuration, the other bulb would go out. This is not true for the parallel configuration.

7.   Two identical light bulbs are equivalent to two identical resistors. Power is found from $P = IV = V^2/R$. To obtain the largest power, we want the largest possible V together with the smallest possible R. We get the largest V by connecting the batteries in series and the smallest R by connecting the resistors (light bulbs) in parallel. Therefore, we get the largest power out by connecting the batteries in series to the light bulbs connected in parallel to form a closed circuit.

8.   The first rule states that the sum of the currents into a junction is equal to the sum of currents out of a junction. Over a time interval Δt, the product of one of the currents into the junction and Δt is the amount of charge that has been carried into the junction by that current. The sum of the currents into a junction times Δt is the amount of charge carried into the junction during that interval. Likewise, the sum of the currents out of the junction times Δt gives the total amount of charge carried out of the junction during the same time interval. Hence, the amount of charge into the junction is equal to the amount of charge out of the junction.

9.   Kirchhoff's second rule states that the gains and losses of potential around a closed loop is zero. Since the potential difference between two points is the difference in electric potential energy divided by the charge moving between the points, a test charge moving around the loop will gain and lose energy as the potential rises or drops. Hence, the total energy of the test charge is the same when it ends the traverse as when it started, i.e., it is conserved.

10.   Since room circuits are wired in parallel, adding a resistor decreases the resistance of the circuit. More current will flow into this branch, and the 100 W lamp will light. Specifically, a bulb's resistance on a 120 V circuit is related to the listed power P by $R = V^2/P = (120 \text{ V})^2/P$. The 60 W bulb has a resistance $R_{60} = 240 \ \Omega$, and the 100 W bulb has a resistance $R_{100} = 144 \ \Omega$. If the bulbs are in parallel, the circuit resistance becomes $R_{eq} = R_{60} R_{100}/(R_{60} + R_{100}) = (240 \ \Omega)(144 \ \Omega)/384 \ \Omega = 90 \ \Omega$.

11.   a) remains the same (it is just the emf)

        b) increases (the circuit current I_1 decreases, so the IR drop across the ammeter and the source of emf decreases)

        c) decreases (the circuit current I_1 decreases)

        d) increases (the equivalent resistance of the parallel resistors 2 and 3 decreases)

        e) increases

        f) decreases (since $I_2 R_2 = I_3 R_3$)

11., continued

   g) decreases (the equivalent resistance of the parallel resistors 4, 5, and 6 increases, so I_1, and thus, I_2 and I_3 decrease)

   h) decreases

   i) remains the same (refer to (b) above)

12.   Batteries are connected in series to increase the available emf, which increases the current through a resistor.

Batteries are connected in parallel to increase the available total charge at the given voltage. Alternatively, we could say that this arrangement provides the same current as one battery (since the voltage is the same) for a longer time interval.

It does not matter in the series case whether the batteries are identical, but it does matter in the parallel case. In the latter situation, currents may flow backwards through some batteries. This can be used to recharge the batteries as the current flows backwards, but can be dangerous if the batteries are not rechargeable, because hydrogen is produced. Hydrogen can be ignited by a spark, and can also cause distortion of the battery's case.

13.   Suppose that battery B is charging battery A. The current is flowing "backwards" through A. The magnitude of the terminal voltage of A is greater than the emf $\mathcal{E}_A$ because of the emf's internal resistance, r_A: $V_A = -\mathcal{E}_A - I\,r_A$. Clearly, the magnitude of the terminal voltage is given by $|V_A| = \mathcal{E}_A + I\,r_A > \mathcal{E}_A$.

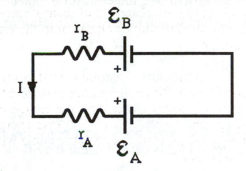

14.   The 18 V emf runs current in the opposite direction to the normal direction in the 12 V battery. If the chemical products produced in the original reaction are still present, this runs the chemical process in reverse, restoring the original reactants. Electrical energy has been converted to chemical energy and the battery has become recharged.

15.   In principle, if we knew the resistance of the external resistor R and the emf exactly, we need only one measurement of the current: $iR = \mathcal{E} - ir$, so $r = \dfrac{\mathcal{E} - iR}{i}$.

However, exact knowledge is seldom the case.

The simplest method is to take an ammeter and two or three or more known resistors. We must assume that there is no temperature dependence for the resistance. First, put in the first resistor and read the ammeter; then the current is
   $i_1 = \text{emf}/(r + R_1)$.
Now add the second resistor in series and again read the ammeter. This time the current will be smaller,
   $i_2 = \text{emf}/(r + R_1 + R_2)$.
(One may do this as many times as one wishes.)

Chapter 19

15., continued

The plot of external circuit resistance vs. inverse current will give a graph that should be a straight line and have as its intercept the internal resistance r. We have assumed that r is independent of current and temperature. Of course, one may solve this analytically as well.

16.   The formula that applies for resistors in parallel will apply (when capacitance is switched with resistance) to capacitors in series. Likewise, the formula that applies for resistors in series will apply to capacitors in parallel.

The potential difference across a capacitor is proportional to $\frac{1}{C}$, while the potential difference across a resistor is proportional to R. Similarly, the charge on a capacitor is proportional to C, while that on a resistor is proportional to $\frac{1}{R}$. When applying conservation of energy and charge to a circuit, C and R have reciprocal roles.

17.   The energy stored in a capacitor of capacitance C connected to a potential difference V is $\frac{1}{2}CV^2$, so in the case that the capacitors are in series, the potential difference for each capacitor will be $\frac{1}{3}$ the emf, for a total energy much smaller than when the capacitors are in parallel, in which case each capacitor has a potential difference of the emf. The factor in energy is $\frac{U_{series}}{U_{parallel}} = \frac{\frac{1}{2}C(\frac{1}{3}V)^2}{\frac{1}{2}CV^2} = \frac{1}{9}$.

18.   The soles of the shoes are made of material that acts as an insulator. When you are in bare feet, your body has a much lower resistance to the flow of current than when you are shod. In this case, current may flow through the low-resistance path to the ground.

19.   Capacitance increases when the separation d between movable plate and fixed plate decreases, and decreases as the separation d increases.

When the capacitance increases, the amount of charge that can be stored increases, so a current will flow and charge the capacitor. This decreases the potential difference across R. The current in the resistor experiences a drop in potential, so that the output voltage drops in sync with the change. This also changes the current in the output circuit, also in synch with the change. Similarly, when the capacitance decreases, the capacitor discharges and the potential difference across the resistor increases. Thus, a current is produced in the output circuit that has the same frequency as the sound wave.

20.   In a charging RC circuit, some of the energy is dissipated in the resistor as I^2R heating. When the capacitor is fully charged and the current stops, the battery will have supplied more energy than is stored in the capacitor.

21.   In an ammeter, the current is shunted around the meter coils to protect them from being destroyed (the coils have a very limited capacity to carry current without "pinning" the meter). The shunt has to have a resistance much lower than the meter, so most of the current travels through the shunt.

In the voltmeter, the current travels through the meter, so there must be a very large resistance in series with the meter resistance in order to limit the current through the meter.

22.   If you mistakenly used an ammeter in place of a voltmeter, the galvanometer shunt resistor (of *very* low resistance so that current will flow almost unimpeded—see the answer to Question 21) would draw a very large current, which could burn up the shunt.

23.   To make the ammeter ideal, we would need to make certain that the ammeter did not affect the circuit at all. Likewise, to make the voltmeter ideal, we would need to make certain that the voltmeter did not affect the circuit at all.

An ammeter is put in series with the elements whose current is being measured. If the ammeter has any resistance, there will be a potential drop inside the meter, reducing the current in the rest of the circuit (see Question 11). Hence, the ideal ammeter should have zero resistance.

The voltmeter, in parallel with the rest of the circuit elements it is measuring the potential difference across, will draw some current if it has noninfinite resistance. This will change the potential differences in the rest of the circuit. Thus, the ideal voltmeter has infinite resistance.

Chapter 20

1.   Earth's magnetic field has a curvature that is different in some places than the ground's curvature. Therefore, it will orient the compass needle along the magnetic field line, which is not parallel to the local ground.

2.   The lines are circles concentric with the wire as shown.

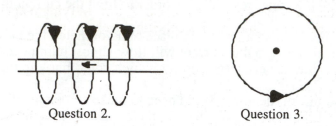

Question 2.   Question 3.

3.   They are concentric with the wire and curl counterclockwise as shown.

4.   A current produces a magnetic field, so the currents in the wires in your house will change the local magnetic field of your compass. If the currents are dc, they may cause your compass to give false readings. If they are ac, they are changing at 60 Hz, and their average effect is zero.

5.   A moving electric charge will carry a moving electric field along with it. The moving electric charge produces a magnetic field.

6.   It will attract only ferromagnetic metals: iron, nickel, cobalt, and gadolinium. It should be noted that some alloys (for example, steel or alnico—aluminum, nickel, cobalt) and composites can also exhibit ferromagnetic behavior. Attraction occurs when the atomic magnetic fields, organized into domains (long range ordering of the atomic magnetic fields caused by interactions among them), are aligned by an external magnet.

7.   No. Only one is a magnet. The other is magnetized by propinquity. Thus, its magnetization changes in response to the large field of the magnet. If both were magnets, one end of the second magnet would have attracted and the other end repelled. Since this doesn't happen, only one of the bars is a magnet.

8.   The field will change as $1/r^2$ near the pole tip, and as $1/r^3$ when far away by analogy with the dipole.

9.   Put the ends of the magnets together in two orientations, in the second of which one bar is flipped. The unmagnetized iron rod will be attracted to the magnets equally in both cases. The magnets will attract in one of the positions and repel in the other.

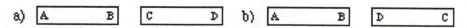

10.   You could make an "electrocompass" by floating a current-carrying coil on a dense liquid and running a current through the wire. The magnetic torque on the coil will rotate the coil until its axis is aligned with the external magnetic field, **B**.

11.   It will feel a downward force. The field **B** is from left to right, the direction of the current is away from your eye, so by the right hand rule, the magnetic force on the wire is downward.

12.   No magnetic force is applied to an electron at rest because $qvB \sin \theta = 0$ if $v = 0$. However, any electron can respond to an electric force. (This question seems to suggest that the fields are turned on separately by someone. A time-varying magnetic field will by itself generate an electric field, which will accelerate the electron.)

13.   Originally, the path of the charged particle determines a plane perpendicular to the magnetic field. If now an electric field points in the direction of the magnetic field, a positively charged particle will be forced to move along that direction as well, and move in a helical path. A negatively charged particle will be forced to move along a helical path turning in the opposite sense.

14.   Imagine a positively charged particle moving to the right in a region in which the magnetic field is down. In which direction is the force? According to the right hand rule, one puts the palm of one's hand flat with fingers outstretched along **v** and curls one's fingers through the smallest angle into **B**. One's palm should be pointing down, the fingers pointing right, and when the fingers curl, the thumb points into the paper. Therefore, the force on a negative charge would be out of the paper.

Now, suppose negative charges flow and the left hand is used. The fingers should be pointing right (the same direction as for the positive charge), and the palm is again down. Curling one's fingers into the direction of **B**, the thumb of the left hand points out of the paper.

One may do this sort of exchange for any sort of motion, so the left hand rule works for the flow of negative charges.

15.   Yes, for one of two reasons:
        (1) the **v** is parallel to **B**, in which case $F_M = qvB \sin \theta$
= 0.
        (2) there is an electric field in a direction so that $\mathbf{F_E} + \mathbf{F_M}$
= 0, which means $|q| \, |\mathbf{E}| = |q| \, |\mathbf{v}| \, |\mathbf{B}|$, and $\mathbf{E} \perp \mathbf{B}$. For example, assume **v** is along x and **B** is along y. Then, if $q > 0$, take **E** along the -z-axis.

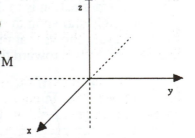

16.   No, because there may be an electric field or a gravitational field in the region of space that causes the motion.

17.   In a region of uniform magnetic field, the KE cannot change. Magnetic fields acting on charged particles can change only the direction of the velocity, not the magnitude of the velocity.

Chapter 20

18.   The wire will create a concentric magnetic field that points toward the reader at the top of the wire and away from the reader at the bottom.

top left (+): **B** is out of the paper, so the deflection is down (using the right-hand rule).

top right (-): **B** is out of the paper, so the deflection would be to the right (using the right-hand rule) if the charge were positive; since it is negative, the deflection is to the left.

bottom left (-): **B** is into the paper, so the deflection would be down (using the right-hand rule) if the charge were positive; since it is negative, the deflection is up.

bottom right (+): **B** is into the paper, so the deflection is to the left (using the right-hand rule).

19.   Magnetic fields cause moving charges to bend. The bright dots on the TV screen are made by electron beams that impinge on the point. Electrons are charged, and so experience a force when a magnet is brought near. This can move the electrons in the beam from their original destinations and cause distortion. A very strong magnet may make a field so large that the electrons spiral along the field lines and never reach the phosphors on the screen.

20.   No. It will make a semicircle as long as there is no energy lost in the region of the field and will come back out in a direction opposite the original one. Actually, there is some amount of energy lost due to radiation from the accelerated charge ("synchrotron radiation"). The displacement of the emerging electron will depend on the electron's energy; the greater the energy, the greater the displacement.

21.   Assuming the fields are uniform, only an electric field (neglecting gravity) can change the particle's kinetic energy. If the charged particle changes direction without any change in kinetic energy, there must be only a magnetic field acting. If the kinetic energy of the particle increases and the particle moves in a helix, both electric and magnetic fields are acting.

If you have the option of reversing the initial velocity of the electron, then the direction of the deflection will reverse for deflection by a magnetic field, but not for deflection by an electric field.

22.   The deflection is to the right. The left to right current in the wire causes a concentric magnetic field shown in the figure that points at some angle to the velocity. The use of the right hand rule shows that the magnetic force will always point to the right no matter how the velocity comes toward the wire (if it is perpendicular as stated). Remember that electrons are negatively charged and so will flip the direction of the force as determined by the right hand rule for positive charge.

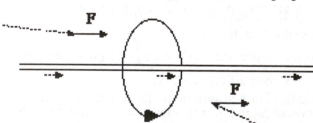

23.   The current I_1 being carried by one wire causes a magnetic field $\mathbf{B}_1$ at the location of wire 2. The field is concentric with the wire and points perpendicularly to the direction of the current as shown. The direction of the magnetic forces exerted by wire 1 on wire 2 are shown in the diagram. At the point of nearest approach, $\mathbf{B}_1$ is parallel to I_2. The net force (sum of the two forces) will be zero.

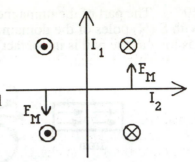

24.   In this case, the top wire is levitated on the bottom wire by the flow of current.

a) The currents are in opposite directions in order to assure a repulsive force between the wires. The condition for equilibrium of the upper (thin) wire is $\mathbf{F}_M + \mathbf{W}_{\text{thin wire}} = 0$.

b) The equilibrium is stable, as pulling the wire down increases the repulsion (restoring equilibrium) and pulling up the wire decreases the repulsive force, allowing the weight to pull the wire down (restoring equilibrium).

25.   The number of loops in the galvanometer, the area of each loop, the strength of the meter's magnet, the stiffness of the spring, and the resistance of the galvanometer affect the sensitivity.

26.   The charge in the semiconductor has been separated, and there is more positive charge on surface a and more negative charge on surface b.

If negative charges circulate in the semiconductor, they leave the negative terminal of the battery and circulate opposite to the direction of (assumed) current flow. Thus, the negative charges move from right to left in the figure. This means that the magnetic force on a negative charge points toward a. This means that negative charge builds up along a, contrary to the measurement.

If positive charge circulates in the semiconductor, the charges move from left to right, and the magnetic force on a positive charge points also toward a. This is consonant with the measurement.

27.   The two ions have the same v regardless of charge. When the ions enter the region of uniform magnetic field in the mass spectrometer, they move in circular tracks with

$$F_{net} = ma = mv^2/R = qvB, \text{ so } p = qBR$$

for both. We may write this as $R = \dfrac{mv}{qB}$, so the singly-ionized ion will end up at twice the distance of the doubly-ionized ion at the end of the half circle path.

28.   The presence of the external magnet will align the iron atoms (and domains) in the unmagnetized piece of iron so that the magnetic fields of the domains point in the same direction as the field of the external magnet. In particular, if the N pole of an external magnet is closest to the iron, then the south poles of the domains in the iron will align so as to face the external magnet. If the S pole of the external magnet is closest to the iron, then the north poles of the domains in the iron will align so as to face the external magnet. Either case produces attraction. This is analogous to electrostatic induction (see Question 16-4).

29.   The part of the unmagnetized metal near a pole will experience domains lining up with S (N) poles of the domain pointed toward a N (S) pole. This makes the nail a magnet (as long as the nail is in contact with the pole). The magnet pole will attract a piece of unmagnetized metal.

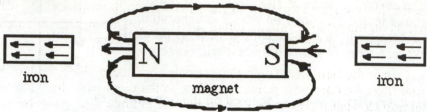

30.   (a) Assume the switch is closed. The bell clapper must be the relay pivot. The steel pivot is attracted to the piece of iron or steel that has been wound with a lot of wire. When the pivot pulls away from the electrical contact, it opens the circuit and turns off the magnetic field. The pivot has a spring to pull it toward the bell. When the pivot strikes the bell, it closes the circuit by touching the electrical contact and the current resumes flow through the coil, turning the magnetic field back on again. The process repeats as long as the circuit is closed at the switch (this switch is the doorbell button you push to ring the bell).

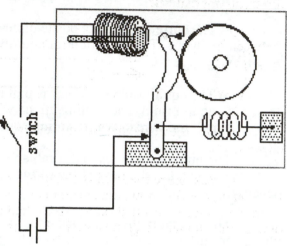

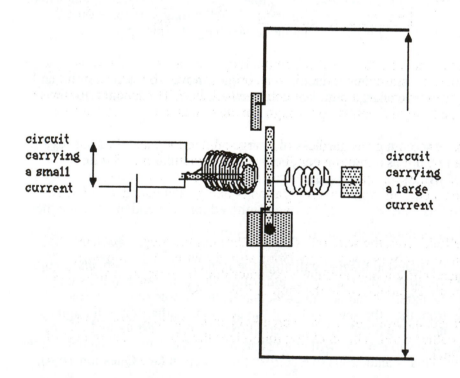

(b) In this case, the loop circuit and the relay are separate. The loop circuit pulls the relay into position. When the relay is closed, a large current can flow through the pivot. Turning off the small current in the windings releases the pivot, which again may be restored using a spring.

Chapter 21

1. The effect is magnified, because each turn independently generates an induced current.

2. Magnetic flux measures the flow of field lines through a surface: $\Phi_B = BA \cos \theta$. Hence, it depends on the relative orientation of the field and the surface. Flux can be zero even for a very large field if the field line is properly oriented (but not vice versa).

3. a) Yes, since the field is changing, a current is induced. Since the loop experiences more south pole flux, the current is induced to flow in the clockwise direction to attempt to return the situation to what it had been. (To oppose the change, B_{ind} must be in the direction opposite **B**.)

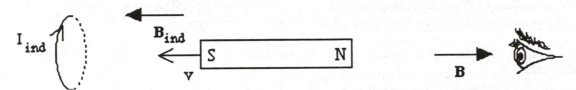

b) No, if the magnet is held steady, there is no *change* in field, so no induced current.

c) Yes, since the field is changing, a current is induced. Since the loop experiences less south pole flux now, the current is induced to flow in the counterclockwise direction to attempt to return the situation to what it had been when the magnet was stationary. (To oppose the change, B_{ind} must be in the same direction as **B**.)

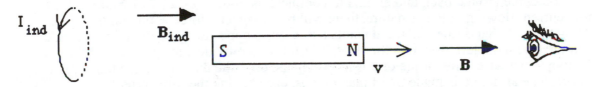

4. If the rod moves to the left, the flux through the loop decreases. A current is induced that will attempt to increase the flux back to its original value. Because the field points out of the paper, the current must circulate counterclockwise. The counterclockwise current makes a magnetic field that points up through the area, thus, increasing the flux.

5. Left loop: There is no change in magnetic flux through the loop and therefore no induced current. (However, this is a moving conductor in a magnetic field. The free charges in the conductor will experience a magnetic force, which will cause a charge separation. There will be a current while this separation is being established. See Ex. 21-4.)

Right loop: The field from the wire points down through the loop. The magnetic field decreases in size as one moves away from a long straight wire. This loop will, therefore, carry an induced current that attempts to counter that decrease, so it will have an induced current that circulates clockwise in the loop in Fig. 21-42.

6. As we have learned, a current in one wire creates electric and magnetic fields that can affect the current in other wires. The shielding minimizes the external disturbance of electric fields on the signal.

7.	The small separation reduces the area of the loop containing both wires as boundaries, and so minimizes induced emfs.

8.	The starter motor engages the flywheel through gear teeth. The starter motor winds one way when current from the battery flows, causing the flywheel to rotate, which compresses the air-gas mixture in the cylinders. The spark can cause the motor to start and keep running. After the car started, the starter motor could run parasitically off the motor, in which case current will flow in the opposite direction. This current could be used to charge the battery.

9.	When an appliance starts, it draws current that didn't flow before. This changes conditions in the circuit, inducing currents. So at the start, the current surge causes the house's voltage to drop, dimming the lights. After the motor speeds up, the back emf in the motor has increased and the motor will draw less current.

Since there is no back emf in an electric heater, the heater will draw a large current as long as it is on.

10.	A rotating motor generates a back emf and, therefore, acts as a generator. A generator providing current to an external load will produce a countertorque and will act as a motor.

11.	There is an induced current being generated by the changing magnetic flux in Fig. 21-12. Suppose we're in the part of the cycle where the right hand side of the loop is rising just after it was horizontal. The loop is experiencing an increased magnetic flux, so a current will be induced to counter the change. It will circulate from the axle to the side near the S pole, then to the back and around to complete the loop (Fig. 21-12). Since there is now current flowing in the armature, there will be a magnetic force acting on the loop. Using the right hand rule, the force points in the sense opposite to the direction the axle is turning: up on the left, down on the right. These forces provide a torque that would rotate the loop clockwise. The torque of this loop is in the opposite direction from the applied torque. The armature is made up of many loops, each having the same effect.

12.	Any metal sheet is a conductor and will experience eddy currents. These occur whether or not the metal is ferromagnetic.

13.	The metals will have eddy currents induced in them by the motion of the pieces past permanent magnets on an incline and, thus, will slide more slowly than the nonmetals. If there are grilles for the small pieces to fall, the metals will be separated.

14.	The slotted bar reduces the size of the eddy currents that can be induced in the bar. The force retarding the metal depends on the size of the flux; a smaller flux means a smaller induced field.

15.	The magnet must be a horseshoe magnet. The sheet is a conducting region. A change in the magnetic flux occurs when one attempts to move the sheet; this generates current loops and induced magnetic field that interact back with the fields. The magnetic forces attempt to return (as Lenz's Law states) the flux back to the original value.

16.   Eddy currents are induced in the tube because the falling magnet produces a changing magnetic environment for the successive "loops" made of contiguous pieces of tube.

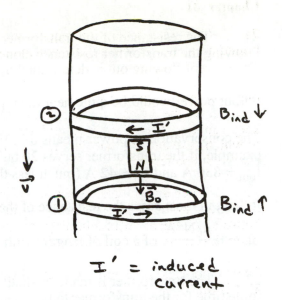

I' = induced current

The north pole of the bar magnet is repelled by $\mathbf{B}_{ind}$ at location 1 and the south pole of the bar magnet is attracted by $\mathbf{B}_{ind}$ at location 2. The eddy currents interact with the magnet, braking its fall, because both produce forces that oppose the downward motion of the bar magnet.

17.   If a metal bar moves in a magnetic field, it will experience a changing magnetic flux, which means the inducing of eddy currents in the bar. The induced magnetic fields associated with the induced currents interact with the original magnetic field to cause rapid decrease in oscillation.

18.   To find out which wires are paired, one may simply connect a bulb and battery (or a number of batteries in series if needed) through the wires, pairing the wires one at a time. The bulb will light only when the two wires make a continuous path. The two paired wires may be found this way.

Alternatively, one may use an ohmmeter. Pairs of leads with infinite resistance are not connected, while those with finite resistance are.

Having identified paired wires, you can put in an ac voltage in one pair and measure the ac voltage induced in the other pair of wires. The ratio of the voltages gives the ratio of turns: $N_p/N_s = V_p/V_s$.

19.   Higher voltages in the home might mean more deaths from accidental electrocution. This would involve lower currents in the transmission lines, saving energy in transmission, but higher currents in the home (with current types of appliances having the same resistance as now). Hence, there would be much more Joule heating of the wires in the home, wasting some of the savings. Most importantly, this would either require much more substantial insulation covering the electric wires or could cause fires (this was a very real problem in the first years after electricity came into use). If new appliances designed for the higher voltage were purchased, savings would result because currents would be lower in the home, but there would be a large initial expense for conversion.

20.   In principle, yes; however, the loudspeaker cone has a large area to diffuse sound, and so can move a lot of air, while a microphone (with a small area diaphragm) must respond to very small motions. The induced current would be quite small.

21.   The resistance of the transformer is part of the resistance of the entire circuit. Thus, knowing the transformer resistance alone will not tell anything about the current flowing in. The current flowing out is determined by the power being drawn by the buildings served, $P_{out} = V_{out} I_{out}$. With such a low resistance for the transformer, we'd hazard that the output power would be quite near the input power.

The conservation of power means that $V_{in}I_{in} \approx V_{out}I_{out}$, so $I_{in} \approx (V_{out}/V_{in}) I_{out}$. For example, if the transformer serves 20 buildings, each drawing 5 kW at $V_{out} = 220$ V, then $I_{out} = 830$ A and $I_{in} = 42$ A (much less than 24,000 A!).

In fact, in most cases the resistance of the primary is irrelevant because the impedance $X_L = \omega L = \omega \dfrac{\mu_0 N^2 A}{l}$ of a coil of length l with N turns is relatively large, much greater than R.

22.   The transformer is made of small gauge wire wound tightly. The ac cycle allows some time for the transformer to be essentially "off," with only a small current flowing and a small amount of Joule heating. When the current flows steadily, the wires get hotter and hotter, finally melting the insulation and shorting the transformer. In this case also, $X_L \gg R$. For dc, $X_L = 0$.

23.   The coils should be arranged with their planes parallel to one another for greatest mutual inductance. They should be arranged with their planes perpendicular to one another for least mutual inductance.

24.   To make the greatest self inductance, coil the wire as tightly as possible to make as many individual loops as possible. To make the least self inductance, stretch the wire out straight.

25.   (a) No. The circuit is an LR circuit and the time needed to reach a given *fraction* of the current depends only on the time constant of the circuit, L/R.
(b) Since the maximum current is V/R, the time required for the attainment of a given *value* of current will involve V.

26.   Not from this alone. Note that cos ϕ is symmetric about 0 (lead means $\phi > 0$, lag means $\phi < 0$). One needs to study the circuit in more detail. The phase of the entire circuit will involve ϕ.

27.   The magnitude of the net impedance is
$$Z = \left(R^2 + \left(\omega L - \frac{1}{\omega C} \right)^2 \right)^{1/2}.$$
If we fix R and vary ω to find where Z is minimum, it is clear that that will occur at $\omega L = \dfrac{1}{\omega C}$, so $\omega = (LC)^{-1/2}$. Note that I_{rms} is a maximum at this frequency.

28.   The amount of charge in the capacitor oscillates. The current in the inductor oscillates. The energy contained in the circuit oscillates between being stored in the electric field (in the capacitor) and the magnetic field (in the inductor).

29.   The self inductance plays the role of mass ($L\frac{\Delta I}{\Delta t}$ compared to $m\frac{\Delta v}{\Delta t}$) and the inverse of the capacitance plays the role of the force constant ($-\frac{1}{C}q$ compared to $-kx$).

Chapter 22

1.   The magnetic field will oscillate in a vertical plane up and down.

2.   Sound is not an electromagnetic wave. It is a longitudinal pressure wave in air (or other medium).

3.   EM waves can travel through empty space. That is how we get energy from the Sun and how astronomers learn about the universe—by detecting EM radiation both in the visible and radio-frequency range. Sound waves cannot travel through a vacuum.

4.   Both light and sound are waves (oscillations). Sound is a longitudinal pressure wave in air (or other medium). Light is a transverse electromagnetic wave consisting of mutually perpendicular oscillating electric and magnetic fields.

5. $\lambda_{radio} > \lambda_{visible\ light}$
$\lambda_{TV} > \lambda_{visible\ light}$
$\lambda_{visible\ light} = 400 - 750$ nm

FM radio f $\approx 10^8$ Hz, $\lambda = \frac{v}{f} \approx 3$ m.

AM radio f $\approx 10^6$ Hz, $\lambda \approx 300$ m.
TV: VHF, similar f range to FM radio.
    UHF, f $\approx 5 \times 10^8$ Hz, $\lambda \approx 0.6$ m.
Use this question to review the electromagnetic spectrum:

```
                        λ
                long
        radio          |
        microwaves     |
        infrared       |
        visible light  |
        ultraviolet    |
        x rays         |
        gamma rays     |
                short
```

6.   Since the wavelength of a 60 Hz wave is about 5000 km, the phase at a house 200 km away from the generating plant will differ by (200/5000) x 360° = 14.4°.

7.   The time lag due to the electrical signal propagation in the wires to two loudspeakers is completely negligible. Any noticeable time lag is due to the differences in the distance of the listeners from the two speakers, since the sound waves travel much more slowly than the electrical signal. This effect can be noticed at large outdoor concerts where people sitting in the rear hear an "echo" from the front speakers. This can be eliminated by artificially delaying the electrical signal to the speakers in the rear.

8.

λ (m)	$f = c/\lambda$	Type of EM Wave
10^6	300 Hz	Alternating current (AC) - Power transmission
10^3	3×10^5 Hz	Radio waves - just below regular AM band
1	3×10^8 Hz	Radio wave - above regular FM band. VHF TV region
10^{-2}	3×10^{10} Hz	UHF TV, Microwave Ovens, Cosmic background radiation
10^{-3}	3×10^{11} Hz	Radar, Microwave communications
10^{-6}	3×10^{14} Hz	INFRARED - frequency just below visible (~4×10^{14} Hz)

9.   Using a flashlight for Morse Code could be considered an extreme example of amplitude modulation (AM), since the amplitude varies from maximum to zero. The carrier is visible light, whose approximate frequency is 6×10^{14} Hz. It could also be considered an extreme form of FM, since in the off position, the frequency could be considered zero. However, in neither case is there a continuous sinusoidal central carrier wave, which is modulated either by varying its amplitude or its frequency. Perhaps the concepts of AM and FM are not meaningful in this case.

10.   At TV and FM frequencies, reception is generally limited to "line of sight" distances. Thus, signals from transmitters "below the horizon" of the receiving antenna will not be detected and thus, TV and FM stations whose transmitters are a suitable distance apart can use the same carrier frequency. AM signals can propagate along much larger distances, particularly at night, when they are reflected by the ionosphere, and their power must be limited so that distant stations broadcasting at the same frequency do not interfere with each other.

11.   The receiving antenna should be oriented in the same direction as the transmitting antenna for best reception. This follows from the fact that the signal is generated by moving charges along the transmitting antenna, and the oscillating EM fields are transverse and mutually perpendicular. Only if the receiving antenna is aligned with the transmitter will the passing EM wave induce an oscillating current in it.

12.   Waves encountering obstacles larger than their wavelength will be "shadowed" by them; waves encountering obstacles much smaller than their wavelength will pass them with a minimum of disturbance. AM wavelengths are considerably larger than the dimensions of buildings or low hills and hence will propagate beyond them. FM wavelengths are smaller than such obstacles and will be more disturbed by them. See also Question 24, Ch. 11.

13.   Cordless telephones consist of a transmitter-receiver (base-station) and a wireless (cordless) receiver-transmitter. The former must be plugged into a telephone outlet and requires house current, the latter is powered by a rechargeable battery. When a call comes in, the base station sends out a radio signal, which rings the cordless receiver. When the "talk" button on the receiver is pushed, the receiver gets the signal from the base and at the same time transmits a radio signal received by the base, so that a two-way conversation can be carried on with the person who called. Similarly, a call can be initiated by pushing the talk button and dialing a number. The information is transmitted to the base, which is connected to the telephone line, and calls the number dialed. Note that all communications between the cordless phone and the base station are via EM waves.

13., continued

Cellular phones are similar, except that they have a much greater range, and their base station (cell) is not in your house but is maintained by the telephone company and serves many people. Things are arranged so that when you get out of range of one cell, another takes over. In principle, you can travel anywhere (or at least anywhere there is a nearby cell) and carry on telephone conversations.

Chapter 23

1.   The light reflected from the Moon's surface does not come off as a beam, but rather, is diffusely reflected in all directions. The Moon's surface does not act as a mirror, and does not show an image of Earth.

2.   The light reaching Earth from the Moon is not a beam of light (or a pencil) but rather, the light travels from the Moon in all directions. As the light hits the sea, the light reflected from the more distant points on the water surface must have come in at a lower angle to the water surface in order to be reflected into the camera (or eye). This light appears higher due to the mirror-like (specular) reflection (in the image of the camera) than the light that comes in closer to the observer (see diagram). These rays would give a circular image of the Moon on the film.

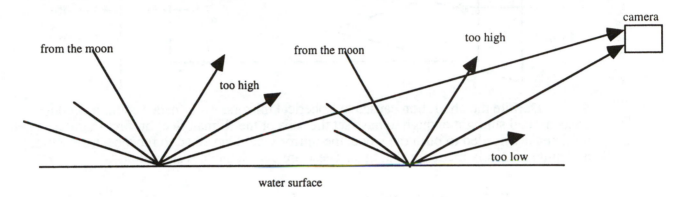

The fact that the sea's surface is not mirror-smooth means that the reflected rays from many places along the water surface reflect light into the camera. The Moon's reflection is more an ellipse than a circle.

3.   Because light travels in straight lines, and the mirror reflects light at the angle of reflection equal to the angle of incidence, we can see that the object seems to be coming from behind the mirror, according to the rays that reach the position of the eye. What's up comes into the eye as up. What was on the right seems to have come from the left side of whatever's behind the mirror. Both result from light reflected from the object traveling in straight lines. See the drawing on the next page for a schematic view of this.

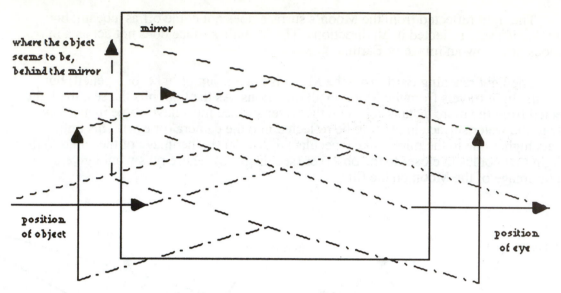

where the object
seems to be,
behind the mirror

mirror

position
of object

position
of eye

4.   Despite the aberration caused by spherical mirrors, Archimedes could indeed have concentrated sunlight enough to have set the sails of the Roman fleet on fire. In order to get the intensity needed to burn the wood, the mirror would have had to have been very big, and quite precisely made for that time. These are questionable assumptions.

5.   Fig. 23-15 shows that this is the case. From $\frac{1}{d_o} + \frac{1}{d_i} = \frac{1}{f}$, one finds $\frac{d_o}{d_i} = \frac{f}{d_o-f}$. A real image is produced when $d_o > f$. Thus, $\frac{d_o}{d_i} > 0$, which means the image is inverted.

(Note: The magnification $m = -\frac{d_i}{d_o}$ is negative for an inverted image.)

6.   To form a real image, the rays of light must reconstruct the image in space at the position of the screen (or eye). The pictures of Fig. 23-14 or 23-15 show the images of objects, but by reversing the rays' directions, they also show that the real image of an object beyond C will be located between C and F. Contrariwise, a real object between C and F will have a real image between C and ∞. If your face is between C and F the image will be past C, and you will not be able to see it.

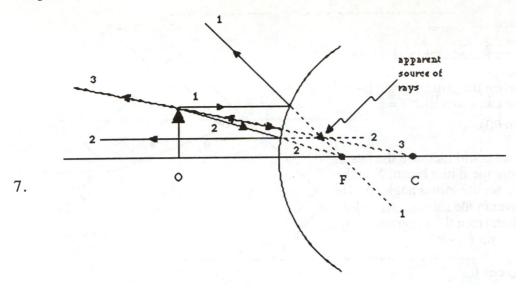

7.

8.   The focal length is the distance in front of or behind the surface of the mirror so that a ray through the focal point will reflect back parallel to the axis. Since all rays hitting a plane mirror parallel to the mirror reflect parallel to the mirror, the focal length is an infinite distance away from the mirror.

There are two mathematical ways to see this. (1) For the spherical mirror, $f = R/2$, and a plane is the limit of a sphere of infinite radius, so $f \to \infty$. (2) For the spherical mirror, $\frac{1}{f} = \frac{1}{d_o} + \frac{1}{d_i}$, but for a plane mirror, $d_i = -d_o$ (virtual image) and so $\frac{1}{f} = 0$ and $f = \infty$.

The magnification is 1, since $m = -\frac{d_i}{d_o}$ and $d_i = -d_o$. We could also say that the object is the same size as the image, so the magnification must be 1.

9.   Yes, since $d_i = -d_o$ and $f = \infty$, Eq. 23-2 is satisfied.

10.   (a) We could measure the angles θ_I and θ_R (see diagram). Then Snell's Law gives $v_I \sin \theta_I = v_R \sin \theta_R$. Thus, $v_R = c \sin \theta_R/\sin \theta_I$.

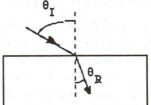

(b) Since the index of refraction is defined as $n = c/v$, where v is the speed of light in the medium, we can send a light ray into the medium from outside until it is totally internally reflected. Then, since the outside medium is air, $\sin \theta_C$ is $\frac{1}{n}$, so $n = 1/\sin \theta_C$, or $v = c \sin \theta_C$.

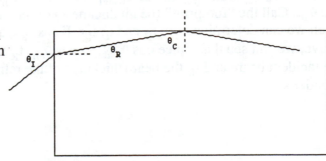

10., continued

Also, knowing θ_I and that total internal reflection occurs (i.e., that no light comes out when the critical angle is reached), we can show that $v = c$ $\cos(\tan^{-1}(\sin \theta_I))$.

(c) Finally, we could measure the lateral deviation from the initial beam, X in the diagram. We set the initial angle, θ_i. The length of travel in the rectangular object is L, say. Then from the diagram,
$$X = L \sin (\theta_i - \theta_r)$$
and so
$$t = L \cos \theta_r.$$

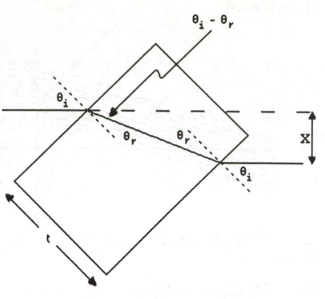

Therefore, using Snell's Law, $n \sin \theta_r = \sin \theta_i$,

$$X = t\frac{\sin (\theta_i - \theta_r)}{\cos \theta_r} = t\frac{(\sin \theta_i \cos \theta_r - \cos \theta_i \sin \theta_r)}{\cos \theta_r}$$

$$= t \sin \theta_i - t \cos \theta_i \tan \theta_r = t \sin \theta_i - t \cos \theta_i \frac{\sin \theta_i}{(n^2 - \sin^2\theta_i)^{1/2}} \; .$$

Overall, we find from this equation

$$v = c \frac{1}{\sin \theta_i \left[1 + \dfrac{1 - \sin^2\theta_i}{(\sin \theta_i - X/t)^2} \right]^{1/2}} = c \frac{1}{\sin \theta_i \left[1 + \dfrac{\cos^2\theta_i}{(\sin \theta_i - X/t)^2} \right]^{1/2}} \; .$$

11.   We know that $n_{air} \sin \theta_{air} = n_{water} \sin \theta_{water}$ and we know that $n_{air} \approx 1$, and that $n_{water} > 1$. Thus, for every ray in the beam incident at the angle θ_{air}, a ray emerges at θ_{water}. The diagram at the top of the next page shows the geometry.

Thus, $\sin \theta_{water} < \sin \theta_{air}$ and so θ_{water} is less than θ_{air}. But if $\theta_{water} < \theta_{air}$, then $\cos \theta_{water} > \cos \theta_{air}$. Call the "footprint" (beam thickness) of the incoming beam on the water surface F. Then we can determine both t_R and t_I: $t_I = F \cos \theta_{air}$; and $t_R = F \cos \theta_{water}$. Comparing with above, we can see that, since $\cos \theta_{water} > \cos \theta_{air}$, $t_R > t_I$. Since t_I is the beam thickness of the incident beam and t_R the beam thickness of the refracted beam, we can see that the beam broadens.

11., continued

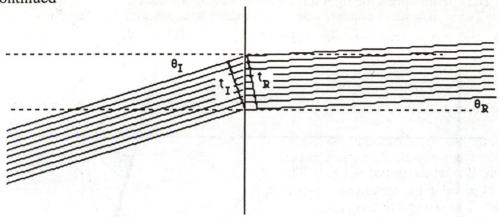

12.   The angle is 0°, since a perpendicular ray is not refracted when it enters a different medium.

13.   The eye thinks the bottom is closer to the surface than it is (first diagram, to the right). In fact, an object on the bottom will appear to be at different depths depending on the viewing angle (the angle between the ray to the eye and the perpendicular to the water surface).

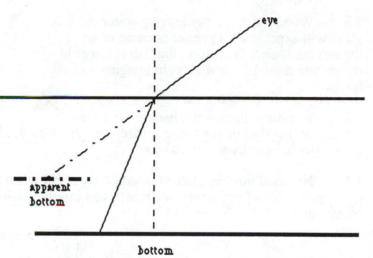

The greater the viewing angle, the shallower the pool appears (following diagram).

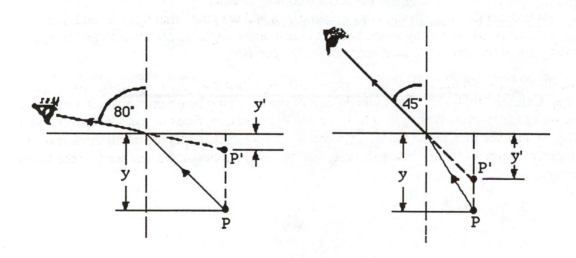

14.   The eye interprets the light it receives as having traveled on a straight, direct path to get to it. The stick always appears shorter, no matter how the stick is oriented.

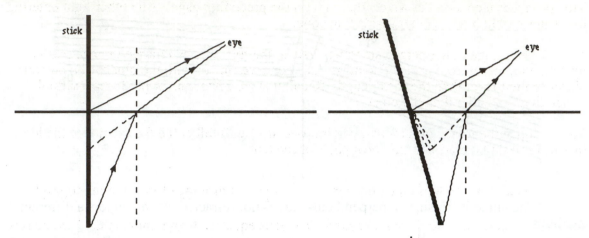

15.   We know that a ray leaving water or glass will experience a greater bending in air than in the water. Therefore, the fish is lower in the picture than the eye and brain imagine it to be.

16.   The drop distorts the background seen through it, making its presence apparent. Light also reflects from the drop's surface.

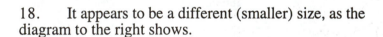

17.   No, total internal reflection may only occur when the light is traveling in a medium of greater index of refraction and reaches an interface with a medium of lower index of refraction.

18.   It appears to be a different (smaller) size, as the diagram to the right shows.

Note also that an eye looking from under the water would see a light ray that made a 90° angle to the surface coming in at an angle determined by Snell's Law to be $\theta_r = \sin^{-1}(1/n_r) < 90°$.

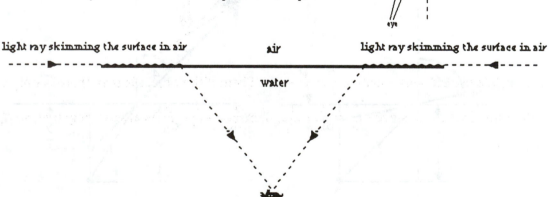

18., continued

This produces a cone in the water (diagram on the preceding page). Any other light entering the water would have to enter inside that cone.

19.   The image of the person standing close to the mirror is an enlarged image that is upright and, therefore, virtual. The mirror is a concave mirror with the object (the person) closer to the mirror than the focal length. Recall that a convex mirror produces a virtual image that is smaller than the object.

20.   Since the image of a far away point (one at ∞) will fall at the focal point of the lens, the film should be placed at the focal point of the lens.

21.   Recall that the lens equation says $\frac{1}{f} = \frac{1}{d_o} + \frac{1}{d_i}$. In moving closer, the photographer has *decreased* d_o, and so $\frac{1}{d_o}$ has *increased*. The lens equation then requires that $\frac{1}{d_i}$ decreases (so that the sum can remain the same). Therefore, d_i has *increased* and so the lens moves farther from the film.

22.   Only in combination with other lenses can a real image come from a diverging lens. For example, one could have a series of lenses produce an "object" behind the diverging lens. Then the "object" is not real and the diverging lens produces a real image.

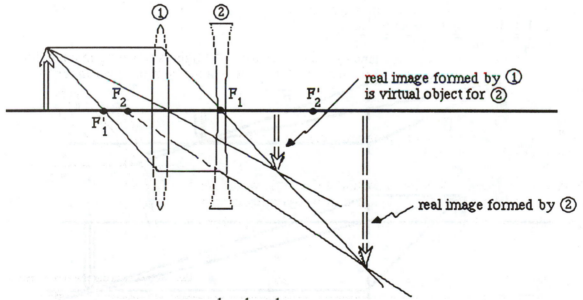

23.   We use the lens equation $\frac{1}{f} = \frac{1}{d_o} + \frac{1}{d_i}$. Then, if the object is real, there is only a virtual image if $f < 0$, since $-\frac{1}{|f|} = \frac{1}{d_o} + \frac{1}{d_i}$, then $\frac{1}{d_i} = -\frac{1}{|f|} - \frac{1}{d_o}$ is always negative, so d_i is negative.

23., continued

If the object is real and f > 0, there may be either a virtual or real image, depending on whether d_o is greater or less than f, since for a real object

$$\frac{1}{d_i} = \frac{1}{f} - \frac{1}{d_o} = \frac{(d_o - f)}{fd_o},$$

which is positive if $d_o > f$ and negative if $d_o < f$.

Since magnification is $-\frac{d_i}{d_o}$, the object is upright if d_i and d_o differ in sign, and upside down if d_i and d_o are the same sign.

24. Yes. If we exchange d_i and d_o, the equation still reads the same.

25. Yes, real images appear on a screen. Virtual images cannot be projected onto a screen, as there is no light in space at the location of a virtual image. One can use a lens system either of the eye or a camera to "see" virtual images and real images, so either may be photographed, provided light reaches the photographic film to form an image there.

26. Yes, the real image changes in both position and size if the object distance is changed with respect to the lens (see picture below). Refer to the lens equation: $\frac{1}{f} = \frac{1}{d_o} + \frac{1}{d_i}$. This may be written

$$\frac{1}{d_i} = \frac{1}{f} - \frac{1}{d_o} = \frac{(d_o - f)}{(f)(d_o)} = \frac{1 - \frac{f}{d_o}}{f} .$$

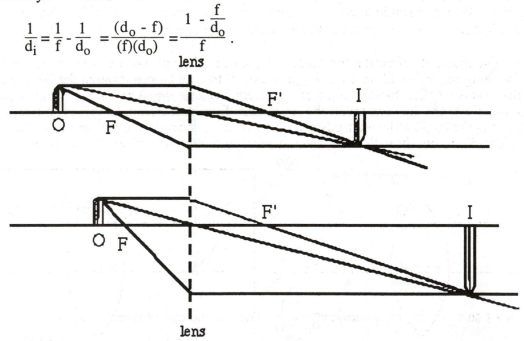

If d_o is decreased by moving the lens, the ratio f/d_o increases, so $\dfrac{1 - \frac{f}{d_o}}{f}$ decreases and thus, d_i increases.

26., continued

The magnification is

$$m = \frac{h_i}{h_o} = -\frac{d_i}{d_o},$$

which increases both because d_i increases and d_o decreases.

27.   The lens equation and the mirror equation appear identical and act in identical ways. These equations are only approximately true. The off-axis rays do not exactly come to a focus at what we denote to be the focal point for either lens or mirror. Hence, neither is exactly described by the lens or mirror equation. The mirror equation assumes that the mirror is small compared to the radius of curvature; the lens equation assumes that the lens is very thin compared to its diameter

Also, because of refraction and dispersion of light traveling in the glass, lenses exhibit chromatic aberration. This does not occur for mirrors.

The object and image distances are both positive on the incident side of a mirror and negative behind the mirror surface. The sign conventions are reversed for image distances for lenses: for a lens, the object distance is still positive on the incident side, whereas the image distance is negative on the incident side and positive behind the lens.

A convex lens is a converging lens ($f > 0$). A convex mirror surface is a diverging surface ($f < 0$). A concave lens is a diverging lens ($f < 0$). A concave mirror is a converging surface ($f > 0$). For a single lens or a single mirror, a real image has $d_i > 0$, a virtual image has $d_i < 0$, a real image is inverted, and a virtual image is upright.

28.   The index of refraction for water is 1.33, so if glass of index of refraction $n = 1.30$ is converging in air, it will be diverging in water. If the ray comes through the air, the angle of refraction is smaller than the angle of incidence, because the index of refraction is greater inside the glass. On the contrary, if the ray comes through water, the angle of refraction is greater than the angle of incidence because the index of refraction is greater inside the water. The diagrams show that the lens is converging in air and diverging in water.

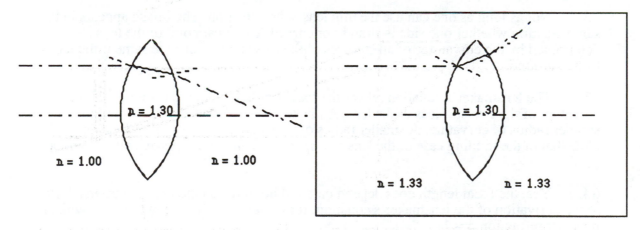

29.   Recall the answer to Question 23-21. In the lens equation, the closer object (the dog's nose) will have a larger inverse ($1/d_o$) than the farther object (the dog's tail). Therefore, the inverse of the image distance will be larger for the farther object (so the image distance itself will be smaller) and smaller for the closer object (so the image distance itself will be larger). As the magnification is defined as $-\dfrac{d_i}{d_o}$, the magnification of the nose will be greater since both the image distance and the inverse of the object distance are greater than is the case for the tail.

30.   An object closer than the focal distance to a converging (convex) lens will produce a virtual image, while an object farther away than the focal distance will produce a real image. If the cat's nose were closer than the focal distance and the tail were farther than the focal distance, then the nose's image is virtual and the tail's image is real. The image of the portion of the cat between its tail and the focal distance would extend (as a real image) from the image of its tail to $+\infty$, while the portion of the cat between the focal distance and its nose would extend (as a virtual image) from $-\infty$ to the image of the nose on the opposite side of the lens.

31.   Look at the lens equation that needs to be satisfied. We have $\dfrac{1}{f_C} = \dfrac{1}{d_{oC}} + \dfrac{1}{d_{iC}}$ (and of course $\dfrac{1}{f_D} = \dfrac{1}{d_{oD}} + \dfrac{1}{d_{iD}}$ also) .

For the case in question, d_{oC} is infinite, so $d_{iC} = f_C$. The image of the converging lens is the object for the diverging lens, so $d_{oD} = -d_{iC} = -f_C$. Then, since
$$\frac{1}{f_D} = \frac{1}{d_{oD}} + \frac{1}{d_{iD}} = \frac{1}{-f_C} + \frac{1}{d_{iD}},$$
the image distance for the diverging lens is
$$\frac{1}{d_{iD}} = \frac{f_C + f_D}{f_C f_D}.$$
This must be positive, and because the denominator is less than zero, so must the numerator. Therefore, $f_C + f_D < 0$, or $f_C < -f_D = |f_D|$.

32.   Not as long as one can use the thin lens approximation. The image appears in the same position whether one side is straight or curved. The focal point of the lens is determined by the curvatures of all surfaces of the lens and remains the same if the lens is turned around.

33.   The lensmaker's equation relates the focal length of a thin lens to the radii of curvature of the two surfaces of the lens. A thicker lens means that at least one side has a smaller radius of curvature. A smaller radius of curvature means a shorter focal length. Note that in the limiting case of the lens as a sphere, the thin lens approximation cannot be used.

34.   Yes, the focal length does depend on the fluid in which the lens is immersed. Refer to the derivation of the lensmaker's equation. It assumed that the lens was in air, with an index of refraction $n = 1$.

The spherical mirror's focal length depends only on the properties of the mirror, since no refraction is involved in its image formation.

Chapter 24

1.   Huygen's principle can be applied to all types of two-dimensional and three-dimensional waves to describe reflection, refraction, and diffraction. Thus, it applies to water waves and sound waves.

2.   Objects placed in direct sunlight become warmer than those in the shade because they absorb the energy of the Sun's light waves and convert it to thermal energy. Since interplanetary space has only a few molecules or atoms per cm^3, energy transport from the Sun to Earth via light waves, not convection or conduction. You can also verify that light waves carry energy by noticing that the side of you facing a campfire becomes warmer than your other side. In the photoelectric effect, to be discussed in Ch. 27, energy from incoming light knocks out electrons from metals.

3.   The ray is drawn perpendicular to the wavefront and indicates the direction of the wave velocity at that location. Rays suffice for describing the straight-line propagation of light when no matter is present and for picturing the change in the direction of propagation on reflection at a surface or refraction at a sharp boundary. On the other hand, to account for interference effects, one needs to use the wave properties of light to find the intensity of the light when two or more light waves reach the same location at the same time.

4.   Destructive interference happens when the crest of one wave arrives at the same time as the trough of another wave. If the two waves are from the same source, this happens if the path lengths differ by an odd number of half-wavelengths.

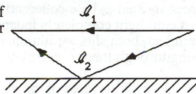

Let $\ell_2 - \ell_1$ = difference in path lengths.
There is destructive interference when $\ell_2 - \ell_1 = \frac{\lambda}{2}, \frac{3\lambda}{2}, \frac{5\lambda}{2}, \ldots, (m + \frac{1}{2})\lambda$, where m = 0, 1, 2, 3, ...

5.   Destructive interference occurs when light that is initially in phase travels through path lengths differing by an odd number of half-wavelengths, while constructive interference occurs when the path lengths are identical or differ by an even number of half-wavelengths: $\Delta\ell = m\lambda$, m = 0, 1, 2, 3, ... In water, the speed of light is smaller than in air. Since the wavelength is the distance a wave travels in one period, the wavelength of light of a given frequency is shorter in water than in air. Therefore, the path difference to produce dark and bright bands is shorter in water than in air for light of the same frequency, and there is smaller spacing between dark and bright bands in the interference pattern.

6.   The distance between adjacent bright fringes on the screen is proportional to wavelength λ (for small angles) and the fringe pattern spreads out more for longer wavelengths. Since blue light has a shorter wavelength than red light, the fringes will be closer together with blue light and the pattern will be less spread out on the screen than with red light.

7.   In a double-slit interference pattern, light from the two slits combines to produce no light (dark bands) at some locations behind the slits. It is very hard to invent a particle model of light which will do this. The diffraction (spreading) of light from a small opening, on the other hand, could be explained by a particle model in which the light bounces off the edges of the opening. In the experiments done in Newton's time, the diameter of the hole

7., continued

was much larger than the wavelength of light, and the interference effects (bright and dark bands) present in the single-slit diffraction experiment were not clearly evident.

8.   Audible sound waves have a much longer wavelength than visible light. The maxima in the double slit experiment occur at $\sin \theta = m \lambda/d$, where d = slit spacing and m = 0, 1, 2, 3, ... If $\lambda > d$, then only the central maximum (m = 0) is present. Therefore, to produce a double slit interference pattern with audible sound waves, the slit spacing must be much greater than for visible light. For example, if the sound waves have a wavelength of 10 cm and the slit spacing = 25 cm, one could detect the m = 0, 1, and 2 maxima.

Because of their longer wavelengths, audible sound waves are easily diffracted around objects that form barriers to visible light. This means that in doing the double slit experiment with sound waves, stray signals (e.g., from reflections off objects in the room) are less easily blocked.

9.   You can't get an interference pattern if the phase of the light from one source is changing randomly relative to the light from the second source. In this case, the light sources are said to be incoherent; this is true of light from two headlights, in which the atoms emit light completely independently. In the usual setup for the double-slit experiment, both slits are illuminated by a single source, so that the light reaching and passing through them is coherent.

10.   At both surfaces of the glass, violet light is refracted more than red light. However, if the two glass surfaces are parallel to each other (as in window glass), then the violet and red beams emerging from the glass are parallel to the incident beam of white light and, thus, are parallel to each other. [Recall that $n_1 \sin \theta_1 = n_2 \sin \theta_2 = n_3 \sin \theta_3$ and $n_1 = n_3$.] The eye focuses parallel light rays onto the same point on the retina. Since the sides of a prism are not parallel to each other, the violet beam emerges from the prism at a different angle than the red beam.

11.   Violet light has a larger index of refraction in glass than red light so violet light is refracted more than red light in passing through the glass lens. This means that the focal length is smaller for violet light than for red light in converging lenses and in diverging lenses (see the figures below). This is called chromatic aberration and is discussed in the next chapter.

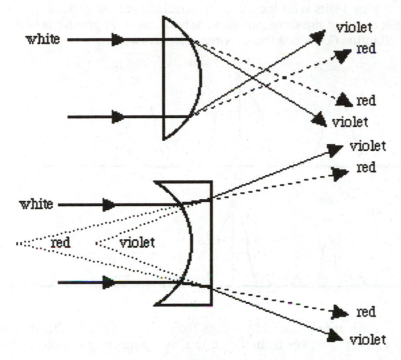

12.   See Question 24 from Ch. 11. If you ignore the effects of reflection from nearby walls, etc., hearing sound around corners depends on diffraction, like receiving radio waves behind a hill. Since the wavelengths of sound in air are very much larger than the wavelengths of visible light, long wavelength sound waves can diffract around obstacles, which cast sharp shadows with short wavelength light waves.

audible sound: wavelengths are cm to meters

visible light: wavelengths are 4×10^{-7} to 7.5×10^{-7} m

13.   Note that the first minimum occurs at $\sin \theta = \lambda/D$. A bigger slit width D makes for less spreading and more closely-spaced diffraction minima, while a longer wavelength has the opposite effect.

14.   Refer to Fig. 24-24 on p. 736.

Provided θ is not a principal maximum, with more slits, there are more possibilities that light from two of the slits will meet out of phase, e.g., light from slit #1 and slit #426 may superpose completely out of phase. Therefore, with a grating, the maxima are sharper and narrower than with two slits with the same slit-spacing (see the picture below). The principal maxima occur at the same positions in both cases. A grating is better for measuring wavelengths (λs) since the maxima are narrower.

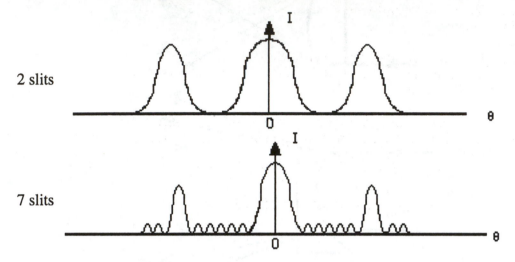

15.   The tiny peaks are produced by waves from a few of the N slits meeting in phase. They are tiny because the waves from the other slits are meeting in out-of-phase pairs.

16.   a) The greater the number of slits, the narrower and brighter the principal maxima will be.
        b) The more closely spaced the slits, the greater the angular separation between the principal maxima, i.e., the more spread out the pattern.

To distinguish between two spectral lines that are very close in wavelength requires (a) a large number of slits so that the spectral lines will be sharp and (b) a small spacing between slits to achieve a larger separation between the lines.

17.   Top color for
        a) diffraction grating: violet
        b) prism: red
In each case, the question is asking which of the visible wavelengths is diffracted or refracted the least.

18.   In interference effects, the difference between getting a maximum and getting a minimum is half a wavelength of light, about 0.25×10^{-6} m, or 0.00025 mm. With a thin film, adjacent bright fringes correspond to a change in the thickness of layer $\Delta t = \lambda/2$. If you try to do a film interference experiment with a piece of glass 1 mm thick, the thickness of the glass would have to be 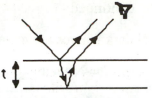 uniform to less than a quarter of the wavelength of light (0.013%), or else the interference effects would wash out (maxima and minima blur together). However, for a soap film which is only 0.00025 mm to start with, variations in thickness of 50% or so will still preserve the interference.

Also, for a thick piece of glass, the reflected beams from top and bottom superpose at the eye only if the angle of incidence is essentially zero. Otherwise, one of the beams misses the eye, as shown in the diagram.

19.   First consider the case of light reflecting from a thin air wedge between 2 flat pieces of glass making an angle θ. For light at normal incidence, bright fringes occur when the path difference $= 2t = \dfrac{\lambda}{2}, \dfrac{3\lambda}{2}, \dfrac{5\lambda}{2}, \dots$, since beam #2 undergoes a 180° phase change on reflection.

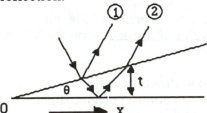

Adjacent bright fringes: $2(t_2 - t_1) = \lambda$, so a change in thickness of the layer between adjacent bright fringes, $\Delta t = \lambda/2$. Since $x = t/\tan\theta \propto t$, the Δx between adjacent bright fringes is constant for fixed λ and θ.

For Newton's rings, the upper surface is curved. We no longer have $x \propto t$. Instead, t increases ever more rapidly than x. Since adjacent bright fringes still correspond to $\Delta t = \lambda/2$, the value of Δx between adjacent bright fringes will get smaller and smaller as x increases.

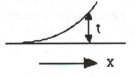

20.   Light that is reflected from the front and rear surfaces of the film interferes destructively at wavelengths corresponding to blue light ($\lambda = 450$ nm) and red light ($\lambda = 700$ nm). This reduces background light from unwanted reflections.

21.   Fill a transparent bottle of length L with air at the desired pressure and temperature and place it in one of the arms of the interferometer. Using a light source of wavelength λ, count the number N of dark fringes that move past a reference line as all the air is then pumped out of the bottle. Light travels twice through the bottle (i.e., forward and back), so the total distance that the light travels in the bottle is 2L. Let N_{vac} be the number of cycles of the light wave in passing through distance 2L after the bottle has been pumped out; then
$$N_{vac} = 2L/\lambda,$$
where λ is the wavelength in vacuum.

Let N_{air} be the number of cycles of the light wave in passing through distance 2L when bottle is filled with air of index of refraction n. Since wavelength in air, $\lambda_{air} = \lambda/n$, one has
$$N_{air} = 2Ln/\lambda.$$

21., continued

If N dark fringes move past the reference point as the air is pumped out, the phase shift is
N cycles. Thus,

$$N = N_{air} - N_{vac} = 2L(n-1)/\lambda,$$

so

$$n = (N \lambda/2L) + 1.$$

22.   As in the case with interference, it is very difficult to invent a particle model of light
that explains polarization effects. Thus, polarization effects are strong evidence for the
wave behavior of light. Polarization indicates that light is a transverse wave.

23.   Sunglasses that are simply tinted do not reduce glare. Polarized sunglasses reduce
glare from reflection off nonmetallic surfaces, such as sunlight reflected from the surface of
a lake or ocean, because light reflected from such surfaces is at least partially polarized
unless the light strikes the surface at zero angle of incidence.

24.   Look through the sunglasses at light that is at least partially polarized (e.g., light
from the sky or light reflected from a nonmetallic object). Rotate the glasses; if the intensity
varies as the glasses are rotated, then the glasses are polarizing.

25.   If Earth had no atmosphere, the sky would be black, since there would be no
molecules in the atmosphere to scatter sunlight. Look at pictures of astronauts on the Moon
as an example, since the Moon has no atmosphere.

26.   There would be more molecules in the atmosphere to scatter the incoming sunlight,
and blue light is preferentially scattered out of the beam from the Sun. Therefore, the Sun
would appear reddish even when overhead, just as it presently does at sunrise and sunset.

Chapter 25

1.   The depth of field is greater and the image sharper when a camera lens is "stopped down" to a larger f-number, because the circles of confusion from the out-of-focus regions are smaller for smaller apertures. Similarly, for the in-focus region, the various aberrations are minimized as the aperture decreases, leading to a sharper image. In the limit of a "pinhole camera," no lens is necessary and the depth of field is infinite.

2.   Question 1 ignores diffraction effects. When the aperture diameter D becomes comparable to the wavelength λ of light, the sharpness of the image becomes diffraction limited, and the angular half width of the central maximum is given by $\sin \theta = \lambda/D$, where θ is the diffraction angle. (Actually, this is true for a slit of width D. For a round hole of diameter D, the relation is $\sin \theta = 1.22 \, \lambda/D$, which is also the Rayleigh criterion for resolution (see p. 776).)

If we take the longest visible wavelength to be 700 nm and a 50 mm focal length lens stopped down to f:22, we get D = 50 mm/22 = 2.3 mm and $\sin \theta = 3.7 \times 10^{-4}$ rad ~ θ. Multiplying this by the focal distance of 50 mm gives 0.019 mm (19 μm) for the "smearing out diameter" of what would be a point image in the absence of diffraction. Even though we have taken the longest visible wavelength rather than a more realistic 500 nm, the diffraction effect would not ordinarily be noticed.

3.   From the lens equation (Eq. 23-8), for a real image, we see that as the object distance, d_o, decreases, the image distance, d_i, increases. Since the position of the film is fixed at the back of the camera, the lens must be moved forward to increase d_i.

4.   In older persons (usually those in their forties), the lens of the eye loses the ability to change its shape to shorten its focal length sufficiently. This lack of accommodation makes it difficult to read or work at normal object distance (25 cm). This condition is called presbyopia and can be corrected with convex lenses for reading. However, if the person is already using corrective lenses (usually concave ones for nearsightedness), the lower portion can be made less concave for reading while keeping the upper portion of the lens for distance viewing. Such a lens, incorporating two different curvatures, is called a bifocal lens.

5.   Most of the eye's focusing is done by the front surface of the cornea, which has a refractive index slightly greater than that of water (1.376 versus 1.333). When a person is underwater, the front surface of the cornea, therefore, cannot refract enough to focus parallel light on the retina and focuses it instead behind the retina, causing the image to be blurred. With goggles, the air-cornea interface is reestablished and the image is focused on the retina.

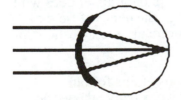
Normal vision
in air

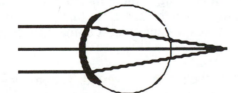
Blurred vision
in water

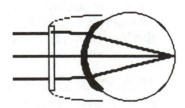
Normal vision
underwater with goggles

6.   It all depends on the amount of correction. Assuming ordinary glasses (not goggles), the water will be in contact with both lens surfaces as well as the cornea. In this case, the two effects will counteract each other. The divergent lenses used to correct the nearsightedness will be less divergent because, instead of air-glass-air media, they now have water-glass-water interfaces, with the index differences dropping from 1.50 - 1.00 = 0.50 to 1.50 - 1.33 = 0.17. This would cause distant objects to focus in front of the retina. However, the cornea would focus less, which in normal sighted people would cause the rays to focus behind the retina (see question 5). Under the right circumstances, these two opposite effects could cancel each other, causing clear vision underwater. In general, however, the nearsightedness would be either undercorrected or overcorrected.

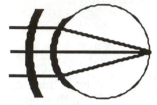 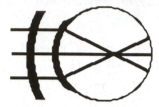 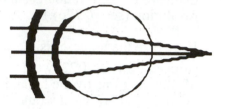

The two effects cancel

Effect of water on lens is greater than that on cornea (undercorrection)

Effect on cornea is greater than that on lens (overcorrection)

7.   Divergent lenses are used to correct the nearsightedness, and convergent lenses are used to correct farsightedness. In the case of the convergent lens, the face is so close to the lens that the image of the face we see must be virtual (of course, the image of the face is guaranteed to be virtual for the diverging lens). Therefore, we see a virtual image of the face through both sorts of corrective lens. The face will be expanded for the convergent lens (think of the magnifying glass, which is a convergent lens). The face will be compressed for the divergent lens. The glasses the person in the question is wearing are divergent and correct that person's nearsightedness.

8.   The film on the camera is passive and will record and integrate any image that reaches it. If the camera moves, both the earlier and later images appear and the result is a blur. The retina, unlike the film, is an active medium and, except for a small time interval called "the persistence of vision," it does not store earlier images but responds only to the instantaneous image. In that sense, it is more like a movie camera than a still camera, except that instead of the discrete sharp successive images on the movie film, the eye forms continuous images. Of course, the brain plays a large role in processing these images (which in fact appear on the retina upside down!).

9.   In squinting, a person is doing something similar to what a photographer does with a camera's f-stop. By closing down the aperture (that is, squinting), the depth of field of the lens is increased. This makes distant objects come into sharper focus. See Question 25-1.

10.   The image formed on the retina is inverted. The implications of this for our perceptions of objects is that the brain plays a crucial role in how we perceive the world.

11.   A simple magnifier and reading glasses both produce virtual, erect, magnified images. However, their purposes differ. The magnifier is used by people with normal (or corrected) eyesight to image an object placed closer to the eye than the near point so that it appears at a comfortable viewing distance (between near point and infinity). Since the object is closer than the near point, it will subtend a larger angle than it does at the near point and will appear magnified.

Reading glasses are used to bring near points which are too large down to the normal 25 cm so that people with presbyopia or farsightedness can read or work at comfortable distances.

12.   The lenses in these toy microscopes are not achromatic and consequently produce chromatic aberration.

13.   Spherical aberration is less if the curved surface comes first. If a plane surface comes first, rays coming in parallel to the axis are refracted only at the rear surface. If the curved surface comes first, these rays are refracted at both surfaces, and spherical aberration is reduced if both surfaces contribute to focusing.

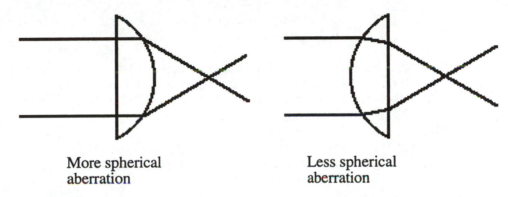

More spherical
aberration

Less spherical
aberration

14.   Spherical aberration is minimized because the pupil diameter is small compared to the focal length (the length of the eyeball). Also, the shapes involved in image formation are not truly spherical. Curvature of field is compensated for by the fact that the retina is curved. Chromatic aberration is minimized because the shortest wavelengths (where maximum dispersion occurs) are preferentially absorbed and because the retina is most sensitive to the middle of the spectrum. One might also consider the possibility that the eye, with its cornea, aqueous humor, lens, and vitreous humor is similar to a compound lens and may be intrinsically achromatic.

15.   Chromatic aberration occurs because different wavelengths of light have different indices of refraction in transparent optical media such as lenses and prisms. The index of refraction does not enter into reflection of light by a mirror and so all visible wavelengths are reflected the same way.

16.   a) Mirrors have no chromatic aberration.
        b) Only one parabolic surface of optical quality needs to be produced.
        c) For a given aperture, mirrors can be made lighter than lenses.
        d) A large mirror can be supported from behind; a large lens can be supported only at its edges and, therefore, sags under its own weight.

17.   The best resolution would be given by the light with the shortest wavelength because diffraction depends on the wavelength. Thus, the resolving power of a microscope is given by 0.61 λ/n sin α where α is the angle of acceptance, n = 1 for air and n > 1 for oil immersion objectives, and λ is the wavelength of the light. Since the resolving power equals the distance between two points that are just barely resolvable, the smaller λ, the better the resolution. (Smaller is better here!) Since the color (measured by f) determines the wavelength (λ = c/f), and the wavelength affects the resolution, the color affects the resolution. So, theoretically, violet light would be the best choice. However, the human eye is not very sensitive to violet light and glass lenses absorb most strongly in that region, so blue is usually used instead.

18.   Atoms have dimensions of about 0.1 nanometers. The shortest wavelength of visible light is about 4000 times greater. It is not possible to resolve objects appreciably smaller than the wavelength because of the large diffraction effects. Thus, visible light can never be used to resolve atomic dimensions.

Chapter 26

1.   You will not be able to detect motion if the velocity is constant. That is the central proposition of relativity, which applies to comoving inertial frames: that the laws of physics are the same in all such frames.

If the train is being accelerated, you can use an accelerometer (for example, a balloon bobbing on a string) to see the effect of this *change* in motion.

2.   The experience indicates that all motion is relative. There is no absolute motion.

3.   If the railroad car is moving at constant velocity, it is just as good an inertial frame as the ground. Therefore, the laws of physics must be the same as for a person on the ground. If the worker throws a ball straight up (as it seems to him), it must come straight down (as it seems to him). We must ignore air resistance (or do the experiment in a closed car), however; otherwise, the man on an open railroad car would feel a wind not felt by a person on the ground. More formally, the ball has the same v_x component as does the car. Since x and y components can be treated separately in projectile motion, the person on the car will see only the y component of the motion, and the ball will land on the car.

4.   The orbital motion of Earth around the Sun requires centripetal acceleration. Therefore, the reference frame of Earth is not an inertial reference frame for treating the relative motions of Earth and the Sun. The first postulate of relativity pertains only to inertial reference frames, so it does not imply an equivalence between Earth orbiting the Sun and the Sun orbiting Earth. If we neglect the motion of the Sun relative to the center of the galaxy, etc., then the center of mass of the solar system is an inertial reference frame. Both Earth and the Sun orbit the center of mass of the solar system, and this center of mass lies within the Sun.

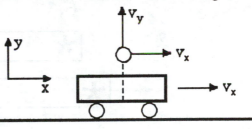

5.   The speed of light in vacuum is measured to be the same by all observers. Therefore, the spaceship observer—you—would find that the starlight passes you at speed c, despite the fact that your spaceship is moving away from the star at 0.5 c.

6.   The first observer (the one who sees both events occur at the same place) measures the proper time interval between events. If this observer finds that the time interval is zero (both events occur at the same time), then the dilated time interval measured by the observer moving at a constant velocity with respect to the first observer will also be zero. So both observers will conclude the events are simultaneous. This simultaneity is only true for simultaneous events occurring at the same place. As the next question shows, it does not hold for spatially separated events.

7.   Observer 1 says that observer 2 is moving to the left with speed v. Observer 1 is exactly midway between A_1 and B_1, and observer 2 is exactly midway between A_2 and B_2. The figures show the sequence of events from observer 1's point of view (the asterisk shows where lightning struck).

a) A lightning bolt strikes B_1 and B_2 at the same time.

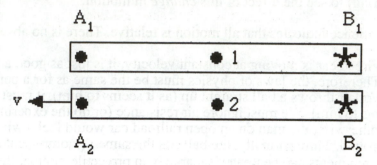

b) A short time later, lightning strikes A_1 and A_2 at the same time (Lorentz contraction is not shown in the diagram; if it were, it would produce spatial coincidence at the A end). The light wave has already left B_1 and B_2.

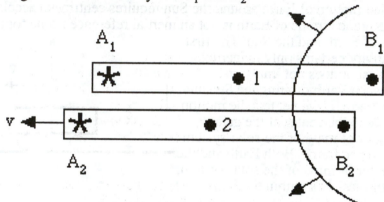

c) The light wave from A_2 and the light wave from B_2 reach observer 2 at the same time, so observer 2 concludes that the two events are simultaneous. However, the light wave from B_1 has already passed observer 1 and the light wave from A_1 has not yet reached observer 1. Therefore, observer 1 eventually concludes that lightning struck B_1 before lightning struck A_1.

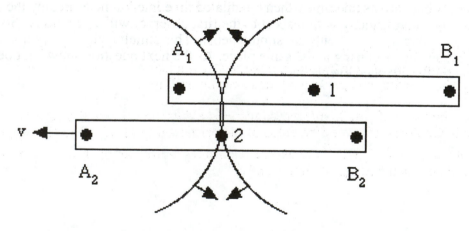

8.   The statement "Moving clocks run slowly" means that time is measured to pass more slowly in a reference frame that is moving relative to the rest frame of the events. For example, the observer who sees both events occur at the same place measures the proper time interval, whereas the observer who sees these same events occur at different locations measures the (longer) dilated time interval.

9.   Since in special relativity there is no absolute reference frame, the phrase "actually passes" can only refer to what you *measure*.

You *measure* Δt_0 if you are in the rest frame of events (e.g., the ticking of a clock).

You *measure* $\Delta t = \gamma \Delta t_0 > \Delta t_0$ if you are moving relative to the events (such as the ticking of the clock).

10.   The astronaut had left her son on Earth and had gone off on a trip in her spacecraft, traveling at a speed close to the speed of light. Her son on Earth concludes that his mother's clock and biological processes run slowly during her trip since she is moving relative to his rest frame. Thus, when she returned, she had aged less than he did. His view of the time dilation is the appropriate one because he remained in an inertial reference frame, whereas her spacecraft became a noninertial frame when it accelerated to take off and to turn around and come back.

11.   Since the laws of physics (and by extension, of chemistry and biology) are the same for all inertial observers, you would not notice any change in your heart rate (relative to other clocks in your reference frame), or in your height or waistline (relative to other rulers in your reference frame), or in your mass. However, an observer on Earth watching you would say that by his standards your heartbeat has slowed, your inertia has increased, and whichever dimension of your body that happens to be oriented in the direction of motion has been shortened.

12.   If the speed of light were 25 m/s, then it would take a great deal of energy to accelerate an automobile from 0 to 20 m/s and it would not be possible to accelerate automobiles to the speeds of 27 m/s, at which cars are presently driven on expressways. Air travel would be impossible because the passenger planes could not reach lift-off speed. Time dilation and length contraction would be readily noticeable.

Two cars with speeds of 20 m/s approaching each other would measure their relative speed as 24 m/s, and one would need to use a relativistic expression to compute the kinetic energy of each car. Telecommunications would be very slow because it would take electromagnetic waves 1.8 h to travel 100 miles = 1.6×10^5 m. Since c^2 would be smaller by a factor of 7×10^{-15}, the energy release in nuclear reactions, $\Delta E = \Delta m\, c^2$, would be smaller by a factor of 7×10^{-15}. Since the Sun is presently powered by nuclear reactions, this change would drastically alter the Sun and could well mean no life on Earth.

Decreasing the value of c to 25 m/s would increase either the value of the permittivity of free space in Coulomb's Law or the value of the permeability of free space in Ampère's Law or both, since $c = (\varepsilon_0 \mu_0)^{-1/2}$. Thus, electric forces would be much weaker or magnetic fields would be much stronger than presently.

12., continued

See George Gamow's *Mr. Tompkins in Wonderland* for a wonderful glimpse of life if the speed of light were small. An amusing science fiction novel, John Stith's *Redshift Rendezvous*, explores some of these ramifications (but neglects others).

13.   At a speed of 90 km/h = 25 m/s, the relativistic factor $(1 - v^2/c^2)^{-1/2}$ in the time dilation, length contraction, and relativistic mass formulas equals $1 + 3.5 \times 10^{-15}$, so these effects of special relativity would be far too small to be measured.

14.   If the speed of light were infinite, we would not have to take into account the time it takes light to reach us, so none of the relativistic effects discussed in this chapter would apply. Indeed, in that case, the relativistic factor $(1 - v^2/c^2)^{-1/2}$ would equal 1.

15.   Suppose an object with proper length L_0 is moving relative to us at $v = c$, and we measure its length L along the direction of motion. For $v = c$, we would find the contracted length $L = (1 - v^2/c^2)^{1/2} L_0 = 0$. If L_0 is nonzero and finite, then having one of its dimensions become zero in our reference frame makes no sense (it is equivalent to saying that the mass of the object has become zero or the density has become infinite). So we conclude that objects of nonzero, finite proper length must travel as $v < c$. A particle of zero or infinite length can travel at $v = c$.

Suppose an object moving relative to us at $v = c$ makes a trip from point A to point B and we measure a finite, nonzero time Δt for the trip. Then in the rest frame of the object, the trip takes a proper time $\Delta t_0 = (1 - v^2/c^2)^{1/2} \Delta t = 0$. Thus, particles traveling at the speed of light (e.g., light or neutrinos) do not age.

If $v > c$, the proper time for the trip would be an imaginary number, which appears to be nonphysical. However, physicists have speculated on the possible existence of tachyons, particles that travel backward in time (making another imaginary factor in such a way that the result *could* be physical). Tachyons could provide communication from the future! Physicist Gregory Benford's famous science fiction novel *Timescape* offers a view of this possibility.

16.   A low speeds (e.g., $v < 0.1$ c), the relativistic mass is constant and the velocity increases linearly with time (acceleration $a = F_{net}/m =$ constant, and thus, $v = v_0 + at$). Eventually it reaches a speed at which the relativistic factor $\gamma = (1 - v^2/c^2)^{-1/2}$ differs noticeably from 1.000. Thereafter, the relativistic mass $m = \gamma m_0$ grows faster and faster, the acceleration produced by the same net constant force becomes smaller and smaller, and thus, the rate at which the speed increases becomes smaller and smaller. The speed approaches $v = c$ and the relativistic mass approaches infinity, but neither reaches these limits. To reach $v = c$ would require an infinite force.

17.   As the iron bar cools, it loses energy. Thus, since $E = mc^2$, its relativistic mass decreases.

18.   Mass is a form of energy that can be converted into other forms of energy; the equation $E = mc^2$ expresses conservation of energy.

19.   The equation $E = mc^2$ applies to all types of particles, i.e., it applies to particles with $v = c$ and to particles with $v < c$. Only particles with no rest mass travel at the speed of light; although such particles have no rest mass, they do have a relativistic mass $m = E/c^2$.

20.   We define the momentum as $\vec{p} = \gamma m_0 \vec{v} = (1 - v^2/c^2)^{-1/2} m_0 \vec{v}$. An upper limit on the momentum can only occur as $v \to c$. Therefore,

$$\lim_{v \to c} p = \lim_{v \to c} (1 - v^2/c^2)^{-1/2} \times \lim_{v \to c} m_0 v = \lim_{v \to c} (1 - v^2/c^2)^{-1/2} m_0 c \to \infty.$$

Therefore, the upper limit on the electron momentum is ∞. Another way to say this is that there is no upper limit.

21.   Because work is done on the spring to compress it, its total energy increases. Since $E = mc^2$, this means that the relativistic mass of the spring has increased.

22.   Instead we say that mass is a form of energy and can be converted into other forms of energy: when a mass Δm disappears, the amount of energy released as another form is $\Delta E = \Delta m\, c^2$. Conversely, energy is converted to mass. See the discussion of pair production in Ch. 27. It may also occur in particle production at high energy accelerators (see Ch. 32).

23.   Our intuition is wrong in fact, but right in effect. Recall that the relativistic velocity addition relation is true as far as we know and can measure. However, at small speeds (compared to c), the effect of the v^2/c^2 factor is negligible, so as a very good approximation, velocities do simply add as vectors (when $v \ll c$).

Chapter 27

1. The higher the temperature, the shorter the peak wavelength in the radiated blackbody spectrum; this is what the equation λ_{peak} T = constant says. (The wavelength at peak intensity of the blackbody spectrum is λ_{peak}). Since the color order of red, yellow, blue corresponds to light of decreasing wavelength, this order corresponds to stars of increasingly high surface temperature. [In all cases the colors of the star are descriptive, since a mixture of all visible wavelengths is present in the light. Your eye responds to an equal mixture of all wavelengths by perceiving the source as white. Although the peak intensity of a star may be in the yellow, for example, the eye will see yellowish-white.]

2. The objects that we can't see in the dark are emitting most of their radiation at wavelengths other than visible, and our eyes are not sensitive enough to detect the very small amount of radiation that they emit in the visible range. For example, an object at 290 K (close to "room temperature") has its peak intensity at $\lambda_{peak} = 2.9 \times 10^{-3}$ m K/T = 10^{-5} m, which is in the infrared, and only a very small fraction of its radiation is emitted in the visible range.

3. The light from a bulb at a temperature of 2500 K appears reddish compared to the light from the Sun. According to Wien's displacement law, the peak intensity of the radiation is at a wavelength of 1.2×10^3 nm (near infrared) for the 2500 K bulb and at 500 nm (yellow-green) for the Sun. In each case, a mixture of all wavelengths is present in the radiation. Sunlight has about an equal mixture of intensities from the violet-blue-green range and the yellow-orange-red range, and the eye perceives this mixture as white. For the light bulb, a greater fraction of the light is emitted in the yellow-orange-red range than in the violet-blue-green range.

4. A blackbody absorbs all radiation incident on it. Radiation entering the small hole in an enclosed cavity reflects around inside the cavity until it is absorbed; at each reflection, some of the energy is absorbed by the walls of the cavity. The pupil of your eye is a hole that appears black for this reason.

5. Indoor light provided by incandescent bulb is yellowish compared to daylight because the temperature of the bulb's filament is significantly less than the temperature of the outer layer of the Sun (see answer to Question 3). Thus, the diamond's color would appear yellowish when viewed indoors. Since the refractive index of the diamond is higher for blue light than for light of longer wavelengths, the diamond will produce greater dispersion of light observed outdoors and thus will sparkle more.

6. A photon of red light has less energy than a photon from the rest of the visible spectrum because it has a lower frequency and E = hf. For the type of black and white film that can be developed in a room lit by a red light, a photon of red light does not have enough energy to produce the specific chemical reaction (dissociation of a silver-containing molecule) in the film. Film that is used for color photographs must be sensitive to red light, so a red light could not be used in the darkroom when such film is developed.

7. A photon at the cutoff frequency f_0 has just enough energy to get the electron out through the surface. The energy required to do this is called the work function W_0. Thus, $W_0 = hf_0 = hc/\lambda_0$. If the threshold wavelength increases when the metal is changed, the threshold frequency and the work function both decrease.

8.   If light is a wave, then there should be no cutoff frequency in the photoelectric effect. If the light wave does not have sufficient energy to eject the electron, one could simply increase the intensity of the light wave and, thus, the electric field of the wave; the larger electric field would give the electron in the metal a greater acceleration, which would get the electron out. Experiments find that this is not the case. Instead, if the photoelectric effect is viewed as the result of a collision between the electron in the metal and a photon with the energy $E = hf$, it is clear that if the frequency is too small, the photon will not have enough energy to supply the required escape energy.

9.   Ultraviolet light has higher frequencies than visible light, so the energy of each ultraviolet photon is larger than the energy of any photon of visible light ($E = hf$). A chemical reaction such as the one which occurs in sunburn requires a minimum energy photon to make it happen. A UV photon has enough energy for this particular reaction, but a visible light photon does not.

10.   When an x-ray photon scatters off an electron, the electron recoils, and thus, takes up some of the energy brought in by the x-ray photon. Conservation of energy requires that the outgoing photon, therefore, has reduced energy. By $E = hf = hc/\lambda$, this implies a longer wavelength for the outgoing photon.

Formally (assuming the electron is initially at rest),
$$hf + 0 \qquad = hf' + (KE_e)' \Rightarrow f' < f, \text{ so that } \lambda' > \lambda.$$
    [Before]   [After]

11.   In the photoelectric effect, the electron is initially bound within a metal or in an atom. The incoming photon is absorbed, the photon disappears, and all of its energy is given to the electron. Part of the photon energy supplies the energy necessary to break the bond (i.e., to do work against the electrical forces to free the electron from its bonds). The remainder appears as the kinetic energy of the electron.

In the Compton effect, the photon is scattered in a collision with an electron, and the photon recoils with a reduced energy. (We consider here the case where the incoming photon has more energy than the electron does initially; the opposite case is often called the "inverse Compton effect.") The photon gives only part of its energy to the electron. In Compton's original experiments, he directed x rays at crystals containing loosely bound electrons; the work function to remove the electron was very small compared to the energy of the x ray, so nearly all of the energy transferred went into increasing the kinetic energy of the electron. The Compton effect also occurs when photons are directed at ionized gases; in that case, the collision is between a free electron and a photon, and all of the energy transferred serves to increase the kinetic energy of the electron.

12.   All of these applications of the photoelectric effect use the fact that the number of electrons ejected per second from the metal plate is proportional to the number of photons with frequency above the threshold that hit the metal plate per second. Thus, the current in the photoelectric circuit of Fig. 27-8 is proportional to the intensity of the light reaching the metal plate and is zero if no light reaches the metal plate. Photocells respond very rapidly to changes in illumination. With a photographic light meter, one is simply reading the current that passes through the ammeter in the photoelectric circuit.

12., continued

When a burglar blocks the light reaching the metal plate in the burglar alarm or smoke reduces the intensity of the light reaching the metal plate in the smoke alarm, the current in the photoelectric circuit drops. In both devices, the photoelectric circuit contains a switch to serve as a relay (see Ch. 20, Question 30 for the design of a relay). When the current in the photoelectric circuit drops, the relay in the first circuit closes the switch in a second circuit, which contains the alarm bell.

In a spectrophotometer, light reaches the photocell after being dispersed by a grating. The photocell is moved to scan across the spectrum. The intensity of the light at each wavelength is converted by the photocell into the electric current in the photoelectric circuit. This current can be used to drive a pen and ink chart recorder.

13.   The evidence for wave properties of light are: interference phenomena (bright bands and dark bands), polarization phenomena, and to a lesser extent the spreading aspect of diffraction. The evidence for particle-like behavior (photons) comes from situations in which light interacts with matter; for example, the photoelectric effect, Compton scattering, and pair production.

14.   The evidence that electrons have particle properties includes the fact that you always see one electron's worth of charge and mass, never less; that you can detect impacts of individual electrons striking a fluorescent screen or a Geiger counter, and can see electron tracks in cloud chambers, bubble chambers, and other detectors; and that electrons obey conservation of energy and momentum like billiard balls in collision situations, such as collisions with atoms or with photons (Compton scattering). You can measure e from the oil-drop experiment and measure e/m from electron deflection in magnetic field. This gives definite value for m. Evidence for the wave behavior of electrons comes from interference effects such as those seen in electron scattering from crystals, and (more indirectly) from the success of theories of the atom which treat electrons as waves.

15.   Photons and electrons both exhibit both particle and wave properties, so the differences must lie elsewhere. These differences include:
    a) an electron has a mass, but a photon does not;
    b) an electron has an electric charge, but a photon does not;
    c) [not studied yet] an electron has spin 1/2, while a photon has spin 1;
    d) [also not studied yet] electrons obey the Pauli Exclusion Principle, photons do not;
    e) an electron has $v < c$; a photon has $v = c$.

16.   Wavelength is inversely proportional to momentum, $\lambda = h/p$. Momentum is defined by $p = mv$, so $\lambda = h/(mv)$. A proton's mass is about 2000 times an electron's mass. If a proton and an electron have the same velocity, the proton has the higher momentum, and therefore, the shorter wavelength:

$$\frac{\lambda_p}{\lambda_e} = \frac{m_e v_e}{m_p v_p} = \frac{m_e}{m_p} < 1.$$

17.   Since the nucleus (positively charged) and the electrons (negatively charged) have opposite signs of electric charge, the attractive Coulomb force keeps the electrons from flying out into space. It thus plays the same role as the gravitational force in the solar system.

18.   If the atoms or molecules are far apart such that interactions between neighboring atoms or molecules can be neglected, then the spectrum emitted is a line spectrum; otherwise, it is a continuous spectrum. Rarefied gases emit a line spectrum. Dense gases, liquids, and solids emit a continuous spectrum. The solar spectrum is comprised of a line spectrum from the rarefied gases in the outer layers, plus a continuous spectrum from the denser gas in the deeper layers.

19.   An almost correct answer is that all the electrons are in the ground state at room temperatures. A fully correct answer requires more care. Electromagnetic radiation is emitted when an electron in an atom makes a transition downward from an excited state in the energy level diagram. If we detect no electromagnetic radiation at all from O_2 molecules at room temperature, this means that none of the electrons in the O_2 molecule have been excited above the ground state: there are no electrons in excited states to make the necessary downward transitions. On the other hand, if the question means simply that we see no visible light (rather than no EM radiation at all), then all that is needed is that the electrons are not excited to a high enough level to give off a visible photon when they fall back. Low-lying excited states of the molecule could still be populated, and invisible low energy EM radiation (microwave or infrared photons) could still be emitted.

20.   You can decide if there is oxygen in the Sun by looking for the set of the spectral lines characteristic of oxygen or of molecules containing oxygen. The spectral lines in the solar spectrum are seen as absorption lines produced by atoms and molecules in the sun's cooler outer layers.

21.   The Lyman series in hydrogen corresponds to transitions down to, or up from, the ground state. If only Lyman absorption lines are seen when a wide spectrum of EM radiation is passed through hydrogen, this implies that nearly all the electrons are in the ground state. If any absorption had been seen at wavelengths corresponding to the Balmer series, on the other hand, this would imply a substantial fraction of electrons populating the first excited state.

22.   The Balmer lines are emitted when an electron in a hydrogen atom makes a transition to the $n = 2$ state from a higher discrete energy level E_n ($n > 2$). The frequency of the spectral line is $(E_n - E_2)/h$. The energy levels in a hydrogen atom are $E_n = -13.6$ eV$/n^2$. The energy levels get closer together as n increases and are closely spaced for large values of n, as near the top of Fig. 27-32. Therefore, as n increases, the energy differences $(E_n - E_2)$ get closer together and are closely spaced for large values of n. This means that the frequencies of the spectral lines get closer together as n increases and are closely spaced for large values of n, as displayed in Fig. 27-27.

23.   In Bohr's model, in contrast to Rutherford's model,
        a) electrons undergoing centripetal acceleration as they orbit the atomic nucleus do NOT radiate unless they change energy states;
        b) energy and angular momentum are quantized, i.e., can take only certain discrete values.
        c) the size of the atom is predicted.

24.   Each of the two electrons is attracted by the charge of +2e on the helium nucleus and repelled by the charge -e of the other electron. We assume that the two electrons are, on the average, on opposite sides of the nucleus. Then the electrical attraction of the nucleus on each electron is stronger than the repulsion between the electrons, so we conclude that on the average, the electrons in the ground state of a helium atom are closer to the nucleus than the electrons in the ground state of a hydrogen atom.

25.   The electron in the hydrogen atom can be in any one of a nearly infinite number of quantized energy levels and still remain part of the atom. A spectral line is emitted when the electron makes a transition from one discrete energy level to another discrete energy level of lower energy, and the frequency of the spectral line equals the difference between the two energy levels divided by Planck's constant. Suppose one views the radiation from a collection of many hydrogen atoms with the electrons in different hydrogen atoms excited to any of large number of different energy levels (i.e., not all of the electrons are in the same few energy levels). Then the spectrum will contain a large number of spectral lines, since each pair of energy levels corresponds to a different frequency and, thus, to a different spectral line. The different spectral lines are produced by different hydrogen atoms.

26.   The Lyman series of hydrogen emission lines occurs in the ultraviolet region of the spectrum. The Balmer series is the only hydrogen series in which visible light is emitted, and thus, the Balmer emission lines could be seen directly by the human eye, whereas detection of the Lyman emission lines required the invention of photographic techniques or other devices for detecting and measuring ultraviolet radiation.

27.   Light of wavelength 89 nm can be absorbed by hydrogen when an electron makes a transition from a bound state to one of the free states above the E = 0 level. The energy levels with E > 0 are continuous rather than discrete. The absorption of an 89 nm photon would produce a photoelectric effect in hydrogen. Light from the sun is absorbed at this frequency but not as a spectral line. It appears as absorption over a continuous range of wavelengths below ("shortwards of") the Lyman limit.

28.   To conserve momentum, the atom must recoil in the direction opposite to the direction of the emitted photon. Since the momentum of the photon of frequency f is hf/c, the atom acquires a speed v = hf/mc, where m is the mass of the atom. This recoil speed is about 0.8 m/s when a photon of wavelength 500 nm is emitted, and the corresponding atomic kinetic energy is 3×10^{-9} eV, so only a very small part of the energy difference between the upper and lower energy states of the electron goes into supplying the very small kinetic energy acquired by the atom. The consequent reduction of the energy of the photon is negligible.

Chapter 28

1.   a) Both a matter wave and a wave on a string *are* waves. The wave on a string, however, is visible to the observer. The only way the matter wave is visible is that the waviness is reflected in the probability distribution of outcomes, because the square of the wavefunction gives the probability that the matter will be at a particular place (or not).

b) Neither the matter wave nor the electromagnetic wave are visible as waves to the observer, but the wave nature of both affects outcomes. Both produce evidence of interference when interference experiments are run. In both, the intensity or the probability distribution exhibit their underlying wave nature.

2.   In Bohr's model, the electron travels in an orbit with a specific, exact radius and an exact value of the kinetic energy (and therefore, of the momentum). However, quantum mechanics says that one cannot know both the position and the momentum of a particle with perfect precision. According to the Uncertainty Principle, there is intrinsic uncertainty in orbital radii (fuzzy orbits) and in the energy differences between levels. Excited states of an atom have limited duration, since they soon decay to lower energy states. For excited states, therefore, the total energy is also not known exactly because of the uncertainty relation between energy and time. According to quantum mechanics, the position of the electron in a hydrogen atom is not well-specified, although it is most likely to be found in the general vicinity of the Bohr orbit for each state. (Quantum mechanics replaces orbits by probability distributions.) Similarly, the momentum (and therefore, the KE) of the electron is not known perfectly, although the E_{tot} = PE + KE of the ground state can be known exactly.

Bohr's model of the atom did not predict the relative intensities of the various spectral lines; all are presumed to have been the same. The relative intensities are predicted correctly by quantum mechanical equations. Furthermore, Bohr's model assumes that there are no states of angular momentum 0, while each atom's lowest state has angular momentum 0 in quantum mechanics (and in nature).

3.   The future position of a particle is predicted from its present position $\vec{x_0}$, its present velocity $\vec{v_0}$, and the net force, $\vec{F}_{net}$ on the particle. Suppose the uncertainties Δx and Δp_x in the x-components of present position and momentum are limited only by the Uncertainty Principle. Since $v_x = \frac{p_x}{m}$, an uncertainty in p_x implies a smaller uncertainty in v_x if m is large.

4.   The baseball is a macroscopic object with a mass measured in kilograms. An electron is a microscopic object with a mass of around 10^{-30} kg. Both are subject to the workings of the Uncertainty Principle: $\Delta p_x \Delta x \geq \hbar$. Recall that $\hbar$ is ~ 10^{-34} J s, quite small. Writing $\Delta p_x = m \Delta v_x$, this means that $\Delta v_x \Delta x$ ~ $(10^{-34}$ J s)/m. Assume in the following that the mass is fixed.

Nonrelativistic objects such as electrons with such small masses may have momenta that are close to order $\hbar$. Thus, for microscopic objects, Δx may be quite large compared to x itself. An electron has a mass about 10^{-30} kg, so $\Delta v_x \Delta x$ ~ $(10^{-34}$ J s)/$(10^{-30}$ kg) = 10^{-4} m^2/s. If the position of the electron is uncertain by one Bohr radius, 5.29×10^{-11} m, the

4., continued

velocity is uncertain by ~ 10^6 m/s. If the velocity is uncertain by 1 km/s, the uncertainty in position is 0.1 μm.

Macroscopic objects such as a 1 kg baseball have $\Delta v_x \Delta x$ ~ $(10^{-34}$ J s$)/(1$ kg$) = 10^{-34}$ m^2/s. If Δv_x is 1 m/s, the corresponding uncertainty in position, Δx, is only about 10^{-34} m, close enough to the exact position! Contrariwise, if the position of the baseball is known to within an uncertainty of a millimeter (a small uncertainty for this object), the uncertainty in its velocity is only about 10^{-31} m/s, which is negligible.

5.   A needle could not balance precisely on a point. Even if the obvious macroscopic disturbances such as air currents, vibrations, earth tremors, etc., could be ruled out, in the long run microscopic quantum fluctuations on the atomic level would eventually topple the needle, since it is in unstable equilibrium.

6.   No, not exactly. The thermometer is a small system compared to the soup, but it is cold and absorbs heat from the soup. The soup transfers some of its thermal energy to the thermometer, and so becomes slightly colder. Both the soup and the thermometer come to an equilibrium temperature that is between the original temperatures of the soup and the thermometer (but much closer to the soup). The act of measuring the temperature changes the temperature, analogous to the act of measuring a quantum system altering it.

7.   Yes, some air escapes in the act of measuring the tire. There is no way to measure the pressure but to let a small amount of air escape out the check valve. The act of measuring the air pressure changes the air pressure, analogous to the act of measuring a quantum system altering it.

8.   Yes, it is consistent with the relation $\Delta E \Delta t \geq \hbar$, because the residence time in the ground state is essentially infinite. This makes $\Delta E_{\text{ground state}} \approx 0$. The residence times in the excited states are finite, so their corresponding ΔEs are finite as well.

9.   The Bohr model predicts that in the ground state of the hydrogen atom, the electron orbits in a plane about the proton with a radius r_0, called the Bohr radius. In the quantum mechanical model, the electron "cloud" (i.e., the probability distribution) starts to fade out at this radius, so that the electron is most probably inside a spherical volume of radius r_0 and, therefore, spends more time near the proton, because there is even nonzero probability for the electron to be inside the proton.

10.   If by size is meant diameter, a factor of three in diameter translates into a volume of $3^3 = 27$ times the original volume into which electrons can be fit. If we then consider that each electron can have two spin states for a given energy level and that these energy levels depend on the electrons' spatial distribution, and that similar correlations hold for different orbital angular momentum states, the fact that over 100 electrons can fit into this volume without violating the Exclusion Principle is not surprising.

11.   The helium atom's nucleus has twice the electric charge of hydrogen and the atom has two electrons instead of one. Therefore, its energy levels differ from those of hydrogen. For example, the ionization energy of helium is more than double that of hydrogen. This produces quite different emission spectra for electrons making transitions to the ground state.

12.   The electrons in sodium circulate about the nucleus, and thus, make an electric current. Electric currents can cause magnetic fields. In this case, the other electrons give rise to a magnetic field that causes the splitting.

13.   Configuration (b) is forbidden because there is no $2p^8$ electron configuration. Only six electrons can be put into a p state.

14.   The uranium atom has 92 protons, and therefore, 92 electrons. The ground state configuration is, using Table 28-3 and additional information to see how the levels fill,
configuration: $1s^2 \, 2s^2 \, 2p^6 \, 3s^2 \, 3p^6 \, 4s^2 \, 3d^{10} \, 4p^6 \, 5s^2 \, 4d^{10} \, 5p^6 \, 6s^2 \, 5d^{10} \, 4f^{14} \, 6p^6 \, 7s^2 \, 6d^1 \, 5f^3$
running total   2   4 10 12 18 20 30 36 38 48 54 56 66   80 86 88 89 92

There is not enough information in the text alone to be able to determine this configuration; the order of the levels must be known far above iron.

15.   a) Since the last shell filled is 3s, it should be in the third period, second column (Mg, 12).
        b) Since the 3p shell is completely filled, we expect this to be in the third period, last column (Ar, 18).
        c) Since the 4s shell is partly filled, this is in the fourth period, column 1 (K, 19).
        d) Here the 2p shell is only partly filled, so this is in the second period, the column just before the last (F, 9).

16.   Sodium: the outermost subshell is $3s^1$. The single electron in the outer shell spends most of its time outside the inner closed shells, so shielding of the nuclear charge by inner filled shells is important. This electron is attracted by the +Ze charge of nucleus and is repelled by the (Z - 1) electrons between it and the nucleus. It thus, "sees" an effective positive "charge" near +1 e. So it is not very tightly bound.

Neon: the outermost shell is a completely filled n = 2 shell, so the electron distribution is symmetric and one does not have the large shielding of the nuclear charge by the inner filled shells that occurs for sodium. Therefore, the electrons in the outermost shell of neon are tightly bound. (Neon: the outermost subshell has 6 electrons in the p subshell.)

17.   Both chlorine and iodine in are the next to last column of the periodic table, indicating that they have a nearly filled p subshell. They lack one electron of a complete shell, and from the outside appear very similar. Since chemistry depends mostly on the outer electrons, the properties exhibited by both atoms should be very similar since the outermost shell and subshell have similar configurations, being filled to the same extent.

18.   Both atoms in the ground state have a single electron in an outermost s subshell, which can be easily transferred to other elements in a chemical reaction. From outside, they appear similar, and their chemical properties are similar.

19.   The rare earths are elements in the Lanthanide series. They are similar because they are filling a subshell with a principal quantum number two less than the outer shell (the greater the principal quantum number n, the farther out the electron's subshells are). The changes in electrons take place deep inside the outer subshell of the atom, leaving the $6s^2$ subshell to be the outer "surface" of the atom for all the atoms. Chemical behavior is similar because the outer "surface" seen by other atoms is the same.

20.   The Bohr model works numerically correctly only for atoms having just one electron. The presence of the other electrons changes somewhat the energies of the transitions from those predicted by the Bohr model. The factor $(Z - 1)^2$ is an approximation.

21.   First, one would change the tube voltage to see whether the lines were stationary because the continuum shape moves, but the K_α, K_β, etc., lines should not change frequency. Measure the wavelengths of the lines to see if they correspond to the expected transitions in the given element. The K_α line results from an n = 2 to n = 1 transition, the K_β from the n = 3 to n = 1, and the L_α from n = 3 to n = 2. Of the K-lines, K_α corresponds to the smallest energy difference and, therefore, the longest λ, since $\lambda = \frac{hc}{\Delta E}$. The L lines correspond to smaller ΔE and thus, have longer wavelengths than the K lines.

22.   The relation between energy and wavelength is $E = \frac{hc}{\lambda}$. Conversely, we find the wavelength from $\lambda = \frac{hc}{E}$. A high energy transition would be what we would expect for a transition from an outer electron level to one of the innermost electron levels, and the higher the energy, the shorter the wavelength. The innermost electron energy levels are influenced by an effective nuclear charge $(Z - 1)e$, with energy levels proportional to $(Z - 1)^2$.

23.   When electrons in atoms are put into excited states, they may remain in the excited state for a time before making a transition to lower energy states and emitting a photon. In spontaneous emission, excited electrons randomly make a transition to a lower energy state and emit photons. Not all atoms are radiating at the same time, with the same phase, or in the same direction. Stimulated emission occurs when light of the same frequency (or wavelength) travels close enough to the atom to interact.

The oscillating electromagnetic field of the incident photon stimulates the excited electron to make a transition downwards. This is a resonance phenomenon. The atom emits a photon in the same direction with the same phase and frequency as the incident photon. The result of stimulated emission from a collection of excited atoms is coherent light.

24.   Laser light and ordinary light both consist of photons. Almost all of the light from a laser is produced by stimulated emission. This means that nearly all of the photons are emitted with about the same frequency, direction, and phase. Because the initial frequency and phase are the same, the photons remain in step with each other as they travel, and so the light is coherent. This makes it useful for producing interference effects, as in holography.

24., continued

Since the photons in a laser beam are emitted in almost the same direction, the laser beam is a one-dimensional, not a three-dimensional wave (i.e., the beam spreads out very little on traveling).

Ordinary light (e.g., from an incandescent light or the Sun) is produced by spontaneous emission. It contains a wide range of frequencies. In such a source, not all of the atoms are radiating at the same time and there are random jumps in phase when one atom "turns off" and another "turns on." Ordinary light is not coherent. Also, since it is emitted in a wide range of directions, the light beam spreads out as a three dimensional wave as it travels.

25.   Light from a street lamp spreads out in all directions. The intensity decreases as the square of the distance from the lamp. You may think of the light from the bulb being trapped in a big spherical balloon. If the radius of the balloon is small, the balloon captures all the light emitted; if the radius of the sphere is large, the balloon also captures all the light emitted. The amount of light captured is the same in both cases. However, since the larger balloon has a much larger surface area, that amount is spread much more "thinly," producing light of smaller intensity. A small area close to a lamp may seem very brightly illuminated; that same small area far from the lamp will be much more dimly illuminated. The laser light is traveling in a straight line and is not diverging much from its position of emission. The laser light, therefore, will illuminate the small area equally brightly whether the area is close to the laser or far away.

Thus, when a laser beam is compared to the light from a street lamp, if the small area to be illuminated is far enough away from the source point (assumed to be the same for the lamp and the laser), the laser beam will appear brighter.

Chapter 29

1.   a) The N_2 bond is covalent (in analogy with H_2, etc.).
        b) HCl has ionic bond—the electron from hydrogen atom spends most of its time
around Cl producing H^+ and Cl^-, which attract each other (see below).

                outermost subshell

H	$1s^1$	$\longrightarrow$	HCl
Cl	$3s^5$		

The electron is easily transferred from hydrogen to make a complete $3s^6$ subshell.
        c) Fe atoms in solid are held together by a metallic bond. ("Free" conduction
electrons and positive Fe ions attract.)

2. $CaCl_2$ could be formed by Ca donating its two $4s^2$ electrons to the two Cl atoms,
each of which needs an electron to complete its $3p^5$ shell, forming as a result ionic bonds
between the Ca^{++} and the $2\,Cl^-$ ions.

3.   Neither H_2 nor O_2 has a permanent dipole moment, since the charge distributions
are symmetrical. This is not true of H_2O, since the shared electrons are more likely to be
found near the oxygen atom. Thus, the region around O is negative, while that around H is
positive; the net positive and negative charges are spatially displaced.

4.   Assuming H_3 is composed of three hydrogen atoms in
the ground state, only two with opposite spins will form a
covalent bond. Since the Pauli Principle says that at most two
electrons can be put into the 1s ground state, the third electron
would have to go into an excited state, raising the total energy of
the configuration. The third electron will be repelled by the other
electron having the same spin. The third electron could go into a
p-state, but that requires more energy and apparently is enough
to break up the H_3 molecule. The H_3^+ ion has only two
electrons and they can have opposite spins and form a covalent
bond strong enough to contain the third proton; the two electrons
would be shared among all 3 nuclei. The diagram shows an arrangement for H_3^+.

5.   Molecular energies can be divided into four categories. Two of potential energy:
strong bonds (ionic, covalent) and weak bonds (Van der Waals); and two of kinetic energy:
vibrational and rotational energies.

6.   Conduction electrons are free to move within the solid sample, which is electrically
neutral. However, removal of an electron would result in a positively charged sample and a
free electron and this would require an energy input equal to the binding energy of the
electron in the metallic bond.

7.   Phosphorus has one more outer electron than silicon and so doping Si with P
produces an n-type semiconductor, because the extra electron goes into the donor level just
below the conduction band, and, at room temperature, goes from there into the conduction
band.

8.   Resistivity of metals increases with temperature because atoms vibrate more rapidly and crystal lattice becomes more disorderly, interfering more with the electron flow and increasing resistivity as a consequence. In a semiconductor the higher energy produced by temperature increase enables more electrons to cross the energy gap between the valence and conduction bands, thus, decreasing resistivity.

9.   A diode can only rectify. It cannot amplify.

10.   During the positive half cycle, A is positive with respect to B and diodes 1 and 4 conduct giving output D positive with respect to C. During the negative half cycle, A is negative with respect to B and diodes 2 and 3 conduct, again giving output D positive with respect to C, thus, giving full wave rectification.

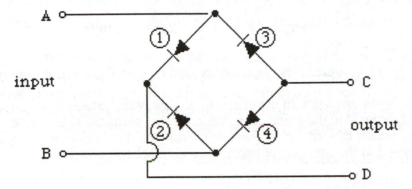

11.   From Fig. 29-31 we see that once the forward-biased diode starts to conduct, its resistance is less than $100 \ \Omega$ and drops rapidly to a few Ω as the bias voltage is increased. From the footnote on page 850, we can deduce that the resistance for reverse bias at room temperature is of order $10^6 \ \Omega$ for germanium and $10^{12} \ \Omega$ for silicon.

12.   A transistor can be used as a switch because a tiny signal current through the base can control a much larger emitter-collector current to the point of either turning it on or off.

13.   If E_c were reversed, there would be no current between emitter and collector because the emitter-base junction would be reverse-biased. (Recall that a transistor can be considered two back-to-back diodes.) No amplification would occur.

14.   Consider Fig. 29-35 with a p-n-p transistor instead of the n-p-n type shown. Now reverse all the batteries. The only change will be in the directions of the currents I_B and I_C, which will both reverse. The amplification will be the same.

15.   Fig. 29-35 shows a working amplifier. The base is at a positive potential relative to the ground, which for this circuit is the negative terminal of the battery. The emitter touches the ground. V_{CE} is shown as larger than V_{BE}, and current flows through the collector to the base, so the base must be negative relative to the collector. The collector-base interface acts like a reverse-biased diode, while the base-emitter interface acts like a forward-biased diode, as may be seen in the picture below.

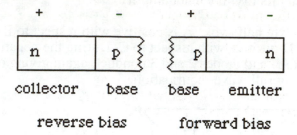

16.   In Fig. 29-36, the bias voltage is produced by using a voltage divider to bleed current from the 12 V source. The capacitor is used to keep DC current from the input.

17.   Diodes and transistors do not obey Ohm's law, which states that current through an element is proportional to the voltage applied across the element. These are extremely non-linear devices, which is what makes them so useful. Another way of looking at these devices is to say that their resistance depends on the applied voltage.

Chapter 30

1.   Different isotopes have the same number of protons, so the atomic number is the same for all isotopes. The number of neutrons differs in different isotopes. As an example, carbon has several isotopes: carbon-12 ($^{12}_{6}$ C) and carbon-13 ($^{13}_{6}$ C) are stable; carbon-14 ($^{14}_{6}$ C) is the best known unstable isotope of carbon.

2.   a) Since Z = 92, this element must be uranium.
       b) Since Z = 7, this must be nitrogen.
       c) Since Z = 1, this must be hydrogen.
       d) Since Z = 38, this must be strontium.
       e) Since Z = 97, this must be berkelium.

3.   The number of protons is Z, given in Question 30-2. The numbers of neutrons is N = A - Z, where A is the mass number. Thus, for
       a) N = 232 - 92 = 140.
       b) N = 18 - 7 = 11.
       c) N = 1 - 1 = 0.
       d) N = 82 - 38 = 44.
       e) N = 247 - 97 = 150.

4.   The periodic table lists the atomic masses averaged over stable isotopes weighted according to natural abundances. In many cases, this makes the atomic mass not an integer because of the presence of two or more isotopes of the same element. For example, boron has two stable isotopes, boron-10 (19.9% of all boron found) and boron-11 (80.1% of all boron found). Thus, the atomic mass quoted for boron is (0.199)(10) + (0.801)(11) = 1.99 + 8.811 = 10.801, neither 10 nor 11. For Cl, with an atomic mass of 35.45 u, the isotopic abundance of A = 35 is 75.8%, while that with A = 37 is 24.2%. There are also small differences from integer values because of the binding energy of the nucleons in the nucleus and the slight mass difference between the proton and the neutron. Atomic mass is defined so that the neutral ^{12}C atom has a mass of exactly 12 atomic mass units.

5.   The protons in the nucleus must repel one another because they are all positively charged. However, it is observed that the nuclei remain together. Something stronger than electromagnetic forces must be at work in the nucleus. Voila! The strong nuclear force must exist.

6.   The differences are more apparent: the electric force is exerted over essentially infinite distances, while the strong force is localized to around 1 fm (10^{-15} m). Only protons among nucleons feel the electric force, while both protons and neutrons are equally affected by the strong force. The electric force is repulsive between similar charges and attractive between opposite charges. At a separation of 1 fm, the nuclear force is attractive between protons and protons as well as protons and neutrons. Electrons are not affected by the strong force. If two protons have a separation of 1 fm, both the strong force and the electric force are much greater than the gravitational force.

There are a few similarities: bonds form from electric forces (chemical bonds) and bonds form from nuclear forces (nuclear binding). In atoms, the electrons fill shells; in nuclei, protons and neutrons fill shells. In both cases, the shell structure results from the Pauli Exclusion Principle.

7.   In α decay and β decay, the original element changes into another element. Also, atomic processes are affected by electromagnetic fields, while such fields do not affect the radioactive decay of nuclei and particles at all. Thus, the lack of increase or decrease in the rate of emission when the materials are subject to electromagnetic fields implies that the processes are not atomic and must be nuclear.

8.   Copper-64 will remain copper-64 if it decays by gamma emission; it will have changed from an excited state to a lower state (perhaps the nuclear ground state). If copper-64 undergoes beta-minus-decay, it emits an electron, so the nucleus must increase its charge by 1 to become zinc. This means that a neutron has changed into a proton, so the mass number remains the same, and the result is zinc-64. If the copper-64 undergoes beta-plus-decay, it emits a positron, and so the number of protons must decrease by 1 and the nucleus becomes that of nickel. Since a proton has changed into a neutron, the mass number remains the same, and the result is nickel-64.

9.   Uranium-238 undergoes alpha decay. An alpha particle is a helium-4 nucleus, and contains two protons and two neutrons. Therefore, four nucleons must be carried away, of which two are protons (leaving 90 protons), and the number of nucleons becomes 238 - 4 = 234. The number of neutrons is $N = 234 - 90 = 144$.

10.   Alpha- and beta-rays are charged and are deflected by a magnetic or an electric field. Gamma-rays are not deflected by an electric or a magnetic field. Alpha-rays are always positively charged, while beta rays can be either positively or negatively charged and gamma-rays (since they are unaffected by electric or magnetic fields) must be uncharged. Alpha-rays are stopped by thin sheets of cardboard, while beta- and gamma-rays go through cardboard. Beta-rays are stopped by aluminum sheets, while gamma-rays go right through. Lead sheets do stop gamma rays. In sum,

	α	β	γ
mass	4 u	m_e	0
charge	+2e	-e +e	0
penetrating ability	small	intermediate	large
speed	< c	< c	c

11.   a) $^{24}_{11}$Na $\rightarrow$ $^{24}_{12}$Mg + $^{0}_{-1}$e + $\bar{\nu}$: If $^{24}_{11}$Na decays by β^-, a neutron must change into a proton, keeping the number of nucleons the same. Thus, the atomic number will become 12, magnesium, and the mass number will remain constant. The result is $^{24}_{12}$Mg.

     b) $^{22}_{11}$Na $\rightarrow$ $^{22}_{10}$Ne + $^{0}_{+1}$e + ν: If $^{22}_{11}$Na decays by β^+, the number of protons must decrease as a proton is changed into a neutron. Thus, the atomic number will become 10, neon, and the mass number will remain constant. The result is $^{22}_{10}$Ne.

     c) $^{210}_{84}$Po $\rightarrow$ $^{206}_{82}$Pb + $^{4}_{2}$He: If $^{210}_{84}$Po decays by α, the number of protons decreases by 2 and the number of neutrons decreases by 2 as well. The atomic number will become 82, lead, and the mass number will be 206. The result is $^{206}_{82}$Pb.

12. a) $^{32}_{15}P \rightarrow ^{32}_{16}S + ^{0}_{-1}e + \bar{\nu}$: If $^{32}_{15}P$ decays by β^-, a neutron must change into a proton, keeping the number of nucleons the same. Thus, the atomic number will become 16, sulfur, and the mass number will remain constant. The result is $^{32}_{16}S$.

b) $^{35}_{16}S \rightarrow ^{35}_{17}Cl + ^{0}_{-1}e + \bar{\nu}$: If $^{35}_{16}S$ decays by β^-, a neutron must change into a proton, keeping the number of nucleons the same. Thus, the atomic number will become 17, chlorine, and the mass number will remain constant. The result is $^{35}_{17}Cl$.

c) $^{211}_{83}Bi \rightarrow ^{207}_{81}Tl + ^{4}_{2}He$: If $^{211}_{83}Bi$ decays by α, the number of protons decreases by 2 and the number of neutrons decreases by 2 as well. The atomic number will become 81, tantalum, and the mass number will be 207. The result is $^{207}_{81}Tl$.

13. a) $^{45}_{20}Ca \rightarrow ^{45}_{21}Sc + ^{0}_{-1}e + \bar{\nu}$: Because this is a β^- decay, one neutron must change into a proton, keeping the number of nucleons the same. Thus, the atomic number of the product will become 21, scandium, and the unknown element is $^{45}_{21}Sc$.

b) $^{58}_{29}Cu \rightarrow ^{58}_{29}Cu + \gamma$: Since this is a γ decay, the atomic number and the mass number remain unchanged. The nucleus changes into a less excited state.

c) $^{46}_{24}Cr \rightarrow ^{46}_{23}V + ^{0}_{+1}e + \nu$: The mass number is unchanged, while the product has one less proton than the original nucleus. Thus, there must have been a positively charged particle emitted, a positron, since the mass number is unchanged, and a positron is accompanied by a neutrino.

d) $^{234}_{94}Pu \rightarrow ^{230}_{92}U + ^{4}_{2}He$: The plutonium emits an alpha particle and changes its mass number by 4 and its atomic number by 2. The product has Z = 92, A = 230. Hence, it is uranium-230 ($^{230}_{92}U$).

e) $^{239}_{93}Np \rightarrow ^{239}_{94}Pu + ^{0}_{-1}e + \bar{\nu}$: The number of protons has changed from 93 to 94, indicating emission of a negative particle. The atomic mass is unchanged, so it must be an electron with its accompanying antineutrino.

14. These electrons will be attracted to the helium nucleus and make a neutral helium atom.

15. When a nucleus undergoes beta decay, one of the neutrons in the nucleus is changed into a proton, thus, increasing the atomic number by one and changing the coulomb attractive force on the electrons. The electrons will rearrange themselves into configurations consistent with the new nucleus, and eventually pick up an electron somewhere in order to make the atom neutral.

16. In alpha emission only one particle is emitted and (except for the energy of the recoiling nucleus) it carries off the total energy of the reaction. In beta emission, two particles are emitted (the electron and the antineutrino) which can share the available energy in many different ways and, therefore, the beta particles show a spectrum of energies.

17.   Electron capture: $^{A}_{Z}X_P + ^{0}_{-1}e \rightarrow ^{A}_{Z-1}X_D + v$. Here, X_P denotes the parent nucleus and X_D denotes the daughter nucleus.

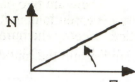

This decreases Z and increases N. Since the reaction must take the nucleus closer to the line of stability in the N vs. Z diagram, the parent nucleus was below the line of stability. The arrow in the diagram shows the result of the electron capture.

18.   Neither hydrogen nor deuterium may emit an α particle because they have too few protons and neutrons!

19.   If a nucleus is radioactive, a collection of such nuclei will decay with a characteristic time constant. After a long enough time, few nuclei will remain because most will have decayed. All naturally-occurring radioactive nuclei present on Earth are long-lived, otherwise they wouldn't still be around.

20.   If the half-life is one month, after one month, half the original sample will remain. After a second month, half this half (one-quarter) will remain. Decay is an exponential, not a linear, process.

21.   The more massive elements are neutron-rich and approach stability by emitting α particles or by beta (β⁻) decay. Only proton-rich less massive elements will decay by emission of β⁺, changing a proton to a neutron. Recall that Z = 83 (bismuth) is the last stable nuclide. Note that if Fig. 30-10, p. 933, is plotted as neutron number vs. proton number, every decay goes downward (toward lower neutron number).

22.   Carbon-14 dating is only useful when there is carbon that was part of a living thing. Stone walls and tablets do not contain the remnants of living carbon, and thus, cannot be dated by using carbon-14 dating.

23.   In carbon dating it is assumed that the metabolism of different living organisms does not distinguish between $^{12}_{6}C$ and $^{14}_{6}C$. Also it is assumed that the cosmic ray flux producing $^{14}_{6}C$ has been more or less constant over the time periods of interest. (The latter assumption can be checked from tree rings for the past 1000 years or so if we make the additional assumption that any fluctuations shown were indeed worldwide, since the tree and the artifact to be dated could literally be half a world apart).

24.   There are two parts to the potential energy curve. Inside the nucleus, the potential energy is essentially zero. Outside, it is given by the potential curve expected for a charged particle, kZe/r, which decreases from a large positive value near the nucleus boundary to zero at infinite separation.

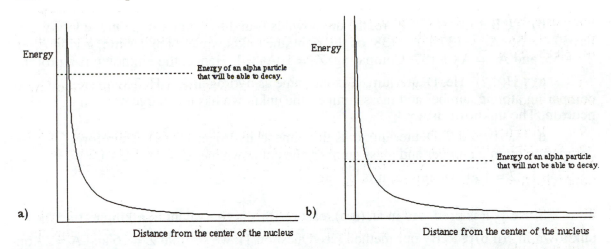

In a nucleus in which α-decay occurs, the α particle must be great enough in energy to be near the narrow part of the potential energy barrier in the nucleus (see diagram a). It will be at an energy much lower down in a nucleus in which α-decay does not occur (see diagram b). The decay is not allowed classically, but occurs through quantum-mechanical "tunneling," having a nonzero probability of seeping through the barrier. Tunneling is much more likely in the thin portion of the barrier than in the thick portion of the barrier.

Chapter 31

1. a) $^{137}_{56}$ Ba(n,γ)?. The unknown is found by thinking about what's happening. A neutron in makes Z = 56, A = 138. The new nucleus has the same identity, but is a different isotope. The γ denotes that the excited state has decayed. Thus, the unknown is $^{138}_{56}$ Ba.

   b) $^{137}_{56}$ Ba(n,?)$^{137}_{55}$ Cs. Here, the unknown is found by comparing. On the left, we have Z_L = 56, A_L = 137 + 1 = 138; on the right ,the unknown and the cesium, giving Z_L = $Z_?$ + 55, and A_L = $A_?$ + 137. Comparing, $Z_?$ = 1, $A_?$ = 1. Hence, the unknown is a proton.

   c) $^{2}_{1}$ H(d,?)$^{4}_{2}$ He. Deuterium, d, is the same as hydrogen-2, $^{2}_{1}$ H. Therefore, comparing atomic number and mass number, the unknown has no charge nor is it a neutron. The unknown is a γ.

   d) $^{197}_{79}$ Au(α,d)?. Deuterium, d, is the same as hydrogen-2, $^{2}_{1}$ H. Therefore, comparing atomic number and mass number, the unknown has $Z_?$ = 79 + 2 - 1 = 80 and $A_?$ = 197 + 4 - 2 = 199. Therefore, it is $^{199}_{80}$ Hg.

2. Since $^{32}_{15}$ P is produced in an (n,p) reaction, this is equivalent to asking to find the unknown in ?(n,p)$^{32}_{15}$ P. By our method (see Question 1), we see that Z = 16 and A = 33 on the right, and thus, must also get this on the left. Therefore, the unknown must have Z = 16 and A = 32: it is $^{32}_{16}$ S.

3. This may be put into the form used in Questions 1 and 2: $^{22}_{11}$ Na(d,α)?. On the left hand side, we have Z = 11 + 1 = 12 and A = 22 + 2 = 24. Therefore, on the right hand side, Z = 12 = 2 + $Z_?$ and A = 24 = 4 + $A_?$. This makes $Z_?$ = 10 and $A_?$ = 20. The unknown must be $^{20}_{10}$ Ne.

4. Since neutrons have no electric charge, they are not repelled by a target nucleus and can get close enough for the short-range nuclear force to act.

5. $^{20}_{10}$ Ne(p,α)?: The reactants are (incoming) p (or, $^{1}_{1}$ H) and $^{20}_{10}$ Ne. The outgoing particles are unknown and α. The atomic number for the incoming reactants is 10 + 1 = 11; the mass number is 20 + 1 = 21. The atomic number for the outgoing particles is $Z_?$ + 2 = 11 and the mass number is $A_?$ + 4 = 21. Therefore, the unknown has $Z_?$ = 9 and $A_?$ = 17. It is $^{17}_{9}$ F. The product is unstable. The reaction is, thus, $^{20}_{10}$ Ne(p,α)$^{17}_{9}$ F.

6. Fission fragments have too many neutrons for the number of protons they contain. They therefore change neutrons into protons by beta-minus-emission (β$^{∇}$emission); that is, by emitting electrons.

7. Yes, because there are more neutrons coming out of a fission than go in to cause the next succeeding fission, meaning that it can be set to give an exponentially increasing number of fissions (a bomb), or it can be put to use as controlled fission. To compensate for having only 1.5 neutrons released per fission, we could use a larger mass of ^{235}U or a more highly enriched fuel or a better moderator to reduce loss of neutrons that escape or are captured on nonfissionable material.

8.   Pu allows a smaller critical mass to sustain fission.

9.   The fission product nuclei, the extra neutrons, and the gamma rays (high energy photons) carry the energy released in fission. By colliding with the lattice of atoms surrounding them, they transfer this energy throughout the material (heating it up). Thus, the thermal energy is that of all the atoms in the vicinity (fuel rods, moderator, heat exchanger, etc.).

10.   Enrichment consists in increasing the concentration of U-235 in a sample of natural uranium, which is composed of 99.3% U-238. Since U-235 and U-238 are isotopes of the same element, chemical reactions will not differentiate between them—they behave in the same way in chemical reactions.

11.   While the kinetic energy of the thermal neutron is modest in the sense that it is nonrelativistic, it is still substantial. Thermal neutrons travel at kilometers per second. The uranium-235 is already unstable because it has an excess of neutrons. The extra neutron tips the system over the edge toward fission. The energy brought in by the extra neutron gets shared among all the nucleons in the nucleus. This puts the nucleus into its vibrational excited state, setting up the oscillations shown in Fig. 31-2. Eventually, a substantial number of nucleons has clumped near the two ends of the nucleus and the nucleus splits in two.

12.   Such an explosion cannot occur now with natural uranium ore (although it could have occurred in the past when isotopic concentrations were greater than 0.7%). We refer here to enriched uranium.
      a) Kept in air: Air is not a good moderator for slowing down the neutrons. The high energy neutrons produced by fission escape into the air, so neutrons are not available to produce additional fissions. So with a porous block, it is less likely that a chain reaction will be sustained.
      b) Kept in water: The hydrogen in the water slows down the high energy neutrons (on collision) to speeds at which the neutrons will be effective in producing additional fissions, thus sustaining the chain reaction. The hydrogen is mainly $_1^1$H but a small percentage is $_1^2$H, which is the best moderator because it does not absorb many neutrons. The $_1^1$H absorbs some neutrons and is converted to deuterium; this (i) removes neutrons from the chain reaction, and, (ii) heats the water. But with a block of sufficient mass, the number of slowed-down neutrons remaining will be sufficient to sustain the chain reaction.

13.   As mentioned in the answer to the preceding question, the function of the deuterium is to slow down the neutrons and allow the fissions to proceed using all or most of the neutrons released in fissions. If the uranium is more highly enriched, there are more fissile nuclei available to break up, and so the loss of neutrons to the surrounding water is compensated for by the increased probability that the neutron will encounter a fissile nucleus.

14.   This was already discussed in the answer to Question 7. If there were less than 1 neutron per fission, the number of fissions would decline rapidly (exponentially). Such a device would be useless.

If there were exactly 1 neutron per fission, and no neutron is absorbed by nonfissionable material or escapes, each fission would be followed by one more, then one more, at a relatively stately pace, neither speeding up nor slowing down. In this case, it would operate continuously (this is the engineered condition in all nuclear energy facilities).

If the effective number of neutrons per fission is greater than 1, the number of fissions will rise rapidly (exponentially). The device would be a bomb.

15.   The energy from fossil fuel is chemical energy, roughly 1 eV/combination. It requires a lot of fuel to operate a fossil fuel power plant. The burning releases noxious gases and particulates, and the gas carbon dioxide (once thought benign, but now known to contribute to global warming). It is expensive to transport great weights of fuel to the power facility, and equally expensive to dispose of solid and liquid waste materials. The burning of coal releases radioactive material (coming from radioactive isotopes mixed in with the coal and decays of such isotopes) into the air. This amount of activity is much greater than is allowed to be released under normal operation of a nuclear power plant.

The energy from a nuclear fission plant requires much less fuel because the energy release is so much greater, about 200 MeV/fission. Some neutrons cause transmutation of elements into their radioactive forms, but American power facilities are contained and releases are small in normal operation. Solid radioactive waste is produced, but it is only about a cubic meter per installed megawatt per year. The depleted fuel is also highly radioactive. This fuel and waste is currently being stored safely at each nuclear facility. When a national repository is completed, the radioactive material will be transported to the repository and stored there for thousands of years. American nuclear facilities have been remarkably clean, but there is some concern that terrorists could bomb a nuclear facility and spread radioactive material widely, or steal fissionable materials to produce a bomb. There is also concern that transport of wastes could cause problems if a traffic accident occurred.

Most energy used on Earth does come from fusion reactions—those in the Sun. The energy from a fusion power facility is still a dream in engineers' eyes, as there will be many years of development needed before these reactions can give energy on a sustained basis. The most likely scenario involves surrounding the reactor with liquid (molten) lithium. This is an obnoxious chemical if released. Also, under neutron bombardment, it can produce nonnegligible amounts of tritium, radioactive hydrogen (hydrogen-3). The energy release per reaction is lower than for fission, but the energy release per mass of reactant is much greater.

All designs use thermal methods to produce the electricity, so all will contribute to local thermal pollution of the air and water in the vicinity.

16.   There are reactors that do use the water that was boiled in the core to run a turbine; these are known as boiling water reactors. The reactor shown in Fig. 31-6 is a pressurized water reactor with a heat exchanger that produces the steam used to run the turbines. This has several advantages: since it runs at high pressure, water reaches a higher temperature before it boils, which increases the thermal (Second Law) efficiency; it also reduces the risk of release of radioactivity to the environment.

17.   The obvious first consequence, since the nuclear bomb was dropped on Japan, obviating the need for an invasion and hand-to-hand fighting, would have been an increase in the number of American and Japanese casualties in World War II's Pacific Theater. There would have been no deaths from the intense heat of the blast, nor would Japanese survivors of the bombings have died in larger numbers than the general population of radiation-induced cancers. Overall, the number of deaths (and certainly American deaths) may have been far larger without the bomb.

More subtly, the absence of nuclear weapons may have lessened the anxiety about the Soviet Union that led to the Cold War and the strategy of Mutual Assured Destruction. One never will know whether the Cold War hysteria would have existed had there been no nuclear weapons.

A nuclear device would have been produced, because the information in the literature was extensive and available. This first device may not have been a bomb, but the knowledge gained would certainly have helped anyone who wanted to build such a bomb. Of course, all this is a guess. No one will ever know what might have been.

Some alternate history science fiction stories have dealt with possibilities similar to those raised here. Among these are C. M. Kornbluth's horrifying short story "Two Dooms," Kim Stanley Robinson's short story of a bomb not dropped, "The Lucky Strike," and Allen Steele's novella "Goddard's People," in which the Manhattan Project money went to fund rocket research instead of nuclear research. Novels of a world in which no bomb existed include Ronald Clark's *The Bomb that Failed*, David Westheimer's *Lighter than a Feather* and Ted Mooney's *Traffic and Laughter*. Ed McKnight from the University of Illinois has been helpful in identifying these stories.

18.   "Hiroshima" stands for the death and destruction visited on people by the device physicists created. After Hiroshima, one famous physicist involved in the Manhattan Project said that physicists have "known sin." It is in this context that the remarks about genetic manipulation are relevant. If the geneticists unleash a "monster," they would have to deal with the consequences for their field in a way similar to that the physicists had to.

19.   Yes, $E = mc^2$, so $\Delta E = \Delta mc^2$ in all those reactions. In fact, this is true for all physical and chemical processes.

20.   In the centers of stars, the energy required to get nuclei close enough so that the nuclear attraction overcomes electrical repulsion is supplied by the high temperature environment. At the center of the Sun, $T = 10^7$ K. At this temperature, only a small proportion of the nuclei have sufficient energy to overcome the Coulomb barrier. But, because of the high density, this is sufficient. (Density is high because of large gravitational force due to the large mass of a star.)

21.   In the central portions of the sun and stars, the hot plasma involved in fusion is confined by the weight of the overlying layers; the plasma is confined by the gravitational force, which is large because the mass of the star is large.

22.   In fission, large mass nuclei with average binding energies per nucleon of typically 7.5 MeV break into two pieces, each having average binding energies per nucleon of roughly 8.5 MeV. Energy is released in the process, totaling less than 0.07% of the matter energy of the original nucleus.

In fusion, two low-mass nuclei, generally with low values of the average binding energies per nucleon combine to produce a more massive nucleus with greater values of the average binding energy per nucleon. In this process, energy is also released because of the difference in binding energies. In fusion, the energy transformed into kinetic energy from matter energy can be as great as 0.8% of the original mass in the case of formation of an alpha particle out of protons and neutrons.

23.   General proximity to alpha particles is not hazardous, as they readily lose almost all their kinetic energy in passing through your clothing or in about a cm of air. In accidentally touching an alpha source with your finger, the duration of the exposure is brief and the alpha particles lose their energy in your skin, not close to vital organs.

Alpha particles that get inside the body may become a problem. When you eat food containing an alpha source, the radiation dose is delivered directly to your esophagus and then over a period of several hours to your stomach (where the effect of the dose can be significant, since alpha particles produce lots of ionizations in a localized region). From your stomach, the alpha-emitting sources may be carried to other parts of your body where they can decay and damage cells, though most are probably excreted (massive metals are excreted especially rapidly), ending the danger of exposure. In machining the metal, metal dust containing alpha-emitting isotopes is released into the air. If you breathe in this dust, the alpha sources get deposited and trapped in your lungs, where they can damage the cells for a very long time.

24.   Inadvertent radiation exposure to pregnant women has shown that the fetus is especially sensitive to radiation. Also, exposure to radioactivity is dangerous because it can ionize particles along its path, specifically components of living cells. Rapidly dividing cells are more sensitive to radiation damage than ones that divide slowly. If the ionized particles are in the germ cells, the exposure to radiation may cause mutations that could be deleterious if the germ cells later developed into a fetus.

Because of these considerations, it is prudent to advise young women who have a high probability of bearing a child at some time in the future to minimize their dose. Older women above childbearing age may suffer personally from exposure to radioactivity, but the effects will not be passed to succeeding generations.

25.   If the pipe carried liquid, for example, it might be treated with a small amount of radioactive tracer dissolved in the liquid. If the pipe leaks, the activity will be detectable by use of a Geiger-Müller counter or some other detection device.

Chapter 32

1.   In an ordinary cyclotron, the frequency necessary to accelerate the protons is independent of radius and equals qB/2m, where q is charge of particle, B is magnetic field of cyclotron, and m is mass of particle. As the energy of the proton increases beyond a certain point, the relativistic mass increase reduces the frequency of revolution and the protons begin to get to the gap too late, get more and more out of phase, and cease being accelerated. In a synchrotron, the radius is fixed and the magnetic field is increased as the particles gain energy.

2. $p + n \rightarrow p + p + \pi^-$

3.   No. Kinetic energy is reference-frame dependent. We can always transform back to the rest frame of the proton and see that it will not decay. If it can not decay in its rest frame, it will not decay in any other frame.

4.   An antiatom would consist of antiprotons, antineutrons, and positrons. On a more fundamental level, it would consist of antiquarks and positrons. If antimatter and matter came into contact, the result would be mutual annihilation, with the final products being gamma rays, neutrinos, and antineutrinos. All of the mass would be converted to energy according to $E = mc^2$.

5.   The appearance of a photon (γ) in a decay signals that the electromagnetic interaction was involved.

6.   Yes. The presence of a neutrino (or an antineutrino) indicates that a weak interaction has definitely occurred. However, not all weak interactions produce a neutrino. (For example, the decay $\Lambda \rightarrow p + \pi^-$ is a weak interaction.)

7.   The decay $n \rightarrow p + e^- + \bar{\nu}$ is a weak interaction because it involves two leptons (the electron and the neutrino) and leptons are not affected by strong interactions. (Note: Just having two leptons in the final state is not enough to guarantee that the weak interaction is involved; the presence of the lepton pairs e^+e^-, $\mu^+\mu^-$, or $\tau^+\tau^-$ in the final state would signal involvement of an electromagnetic interaction, not a weak interaction.) Also, see the previous question. The presence of a neutrino (or antineutrino) itself signals a weak interaction is involved. The small neutron-proton mass difference allows only this reaction energetically. Were it larger, say as large as the pion mass, the neutron could possibly have decayed as

   $n \rightarrow p + \pi^-$.

8.   The table below shows which of the particles is involved with which interaction.

	STRONG	ELECTRO-MAGNETIC	WEAK	GRAVITA-TIONAL
proton	yes	yes	yes	yes
electron	no	yes	yes	yes
neutrino	no	no	yes	yes

9.   Charge and baryon number are conserved for all the decays listed in Table 32-2.

10. Σ^0, π^0, and η^0 decay electromagnetically. This may be recognized because they have gamma rays as one of their decay products.

11.   All particles listed in the table except for Σ^0, π^0, and η^0 decay through the weak interaction.

12.   Note: Σ^+ and Σ^- are not antiparticles of each other, since they both have strangeness ($S = -1$) and their masses are not the same. Their antiparticles, which have $S = +1$ are denoted by a bar above the Σ. There is not enough mass difference between either Σ^+ or Σ^- and Λ for the decay $\Sigma^+ \rightarrow \Lambda + \pi^+$ to occur. However, the decays $\Sigma^+ \rightarrow \Lambda + e^+ + \nu_e$ and $\Sigma^- \rightarrow \Lambda + e^- + \bar{\nu}_e$ do occur. They are both highly suppressed weak interactions. Σ^0 decays to Λ and a gamma ray (γ) via the electromagnetic interaction.

13.   Because the Δ baryon has baryon number +1 and is composed of u and d quarks having charges of +3/2 and -1/3, respectively, and every quark has a baryon number 1/3, the possible charge states are:

   uuu = Δ^{++}, uud = Δ^+, udd = Δ^0, and ddd = Δ^- .

14.   Of the decays shown in Table 32-4 only the decays of the J/ψ into e^+e^- and $\mu^+\mu^-$ and those of the Y (upsilon) into e^+e^-, $\mu^+\mu^-$, and $\tau^+\tau^-$ are electromagnetic.

15.   All the decays in Table 32-4, except for those of the J/ψ and Y (upsilon) occur through the weak interaction.

16.   Baryons are composed of three quarks, each of spin 1/2. If all three spins are aligned (in the same direction), they will add up to 3/2 (1/2 + 1/2 + 1/2). If one of the spins differs from the other two, the spins will add up to 1/2 (1/2 - 1/2 + 1/2).

Mesons are composed of quark-antiquark pairs. Since each quark (or antiquark) carries spin 1/2, depending on their relative orientations, the two spins can add up to 0 (1/2 - 1/2) or 1 (1/2 + 1/2).

17.   This particle could never be detected unless it felt *some* force, even one we have no knowledge of at present. If it did not interact at all with any force, known or unknown, then it could not even be detected indirectly (as was the neutrino initially because of the continuous beta spectrum). No interaction at all means complete decoupling from the universe. Whether something that can never be detected exists is a philosophical not a scientific question. Science deals with the observable, not the unobservable.

Chapter 33

1.   Historically the word "nebulae" (Latin for "clouds") referred to hazy, extended images seen in the night sky with small telescopes. In fact, several very different classes of objects were all being called nebulae. Some of the nebulae are external galaxies. Others are clusters of stars in our galaxy. Others are clouds of interstellar matter (i.e., the gas and dust in the space between the stars) surrounding one or more hot stars; radiation from the hot stars excites the gas cloud so that it glows. Still others are the glowing remnants of a supernova explosion. It required higher resolution observations with larger telescopes and an analysis of the spectra to distinguish between these various classes of objects. In fact, the interstellar gas in the Milky Way does consist of clouds, but except for those heated sufficiently by proximity to hot stars, most of the gas clouds are too cold to be seen by optical telescopes. They are detected through their emission lines in the microwave and radio portions of the spectrum.

2.   Spiral arms are concentrations of interstellar gas and stars in the disk of a galaxy. Gravitational forces are responsible for producing these concentrations. The disk does not rotate as a solid body; instead the angular velocity decreases outward. Consequently, as the disk rotates, any feature extending over an appreciable range of radii in the disk will become a trailing spiral. However, such an arm soon wraps up on itself. Astronomy textbooks describe mechanisms for getting persistent spiral arms. A common explanation involves a spiral-shaped compression wave moving through the disk of the galaxy and triggered either by the close passage of a companion galaxy (pulling material out of the disk on both sides) or by a bar-shaped structure in the center of the galaxy. The compression wave is driven by gravitational forces.

[Aside from pointing out that our Galaxy is a flat disk and showing pictures of galaxies with spiral arms, Giancoli's text offers the reader no clue as to how such arms might form.]

3.   The stellar parallax angle ϕ is given by $\tan \phi = R/D \approx \phi$ (the angle ϕ is given in radians), since $R \ll D$. R is Earth-Sun distance, and D is the distance of the star from the Sun. If parallax measurements were made from a body orbiting the Sun at a distance r from the Sun, then one would be measuring the parallax angle (in radians)

$$\phi_M = r/D.$$

Thus,

$$\phi = \phi_M \; R/r.$$

      a) If M is the Moon, then the difference between ϕ and ϕ_M is negligible, since $R = 1.5 \times 10^8$ km and $|r - R|$ is less than or equal to 3.8×10^5 km. Therefore, no correction would be necessary for astronomers operating from the Moon.

      b) If M is Mars, then $r = 1.5$ R, so the parallax angle measured from Mars must be multiplied by 2/3 to get the parallax angle measured from Earth. One may measure the small parallax angle more accurately from Mars, since the baseline is r, which is greater than R.

4.   Stars are spheres of gas. If a star generates more energy than it radiates, the temperature in its interior will increase. This will increase the gas pressure inside the star. The star will then expand until it is in mechanical equilibrium, i.e., until for every portion of the star, the downward gravitational force is balanced by the upward force from gas pressure.

4., continued

If a star generates less energy than it radiates, the temperature in the interior will decrease. This will decrease the gas pressure inside the star. The star will then contract because the downward force exerted by gravity on any piece of the star is greater than the upward force exerted by gas pressure. As the star contracts, its interior will heat up.

5.   A red giant has a surface temperature of about 3500 K, a much larger radius than the Sun, and a much higher luminosity than the Sun. The low surface temperature results in its reddish color. A star like the Sun becomes a red giant after converting its central core from hydrogen to helium. In a red giant, hydrogen is fusing to form helium in a high temperature shell around the central core. At the red giant tip (the point of highest luminosity during the red giant phase), helium in the central core is undergoing fusion to form carbon. Compared to a star on the main sequence, a red giant has a hotter, higher-density core and a much more extended, lower-density envelope.

6.   The luminosity of a star is
$$L = \sigma A T^4 = \sigma \pi R^2 T^4,$$
where σ is the Stefan-Boltzmann constant (stars are approximately blackbodies), R is the stellar radius, and T is the surface temperature.

       a) In the H-R diagram, suppose a star moves to the left only. This means that its surface temperature increases but its luminosity does not change. Therefore, it must shrink in size (with R proportional to T^{-2}) to satisfy the above equation. Stars going from the horizontal branch to the white dwarf phase initially move on the H-R diagram in this fashion.

       b) In the H-R diagram, suppose a star moves vertically upwards. This means that its luminosity increases but its surface temperature does not change. Therefore, the star must expand with R proportional to $L^{1/2}$.

       c) In the H-R diagram, suppose a star moves to the right and up. This means that its luminosity increases while its surface temperature decreases. Therefore, the star must expand with R proportional to $L^{1/2} T^{-2}$. Stars going from the main sequence to the red giant phase move in the H-R diagram in this fashion.

7.   Theoretical models predict the interior structure of a star and its location in the H-R diagram as a function of stellar mass and age. If a star's observed location in the H-R diagram is compared with these theoretical tracks (such as the one shown in Fig. 33-9), one can deduce what is occurring in the core of the star. In particular, if a star is located on the main sequence in the H-R diagram, then in the core of the star, hydrogen is being converted to helium. If the star is at the red giant tip, then in the core of the star, helium is being converted to carbon.

8.   The mass of the star after the red giant phase determines whether it ends up as a white dwarf, a neutron star, or a black hole. Stars with a mass below 1.4 solar masses after the red giant phase become white dwarfs. A star with mass greater than this contracts to higher densities and temperatures and becomes a supernova. If the remnant after the supernova explosion has a mass greater than about 2 or 3 solar masses, the remnant becomes a black hole; otherwise it becomes a neutron star.

9.   A geodesic is the shortest path between two points. Light travels along geodesics. If the curvature of space-time is not zero, then the geodesic is a curve, not a straight line. In General Relativity, a massive object, such as the Sun, causes space-time and, thus, the geodesics, to curve in its vicinity.

On the surface of Earth, the shortest distance between two points is not a straight line because Earth is a sphere. Airplanes' shortest routes are "great circles," or arcs on the spherical Earth. These arcs are geodesics.

10.   If, in general, the redshift of spectral lines of galaxies were the result of something other than the expansion of the universe, our understanding would change drastically. Before Hubble deduced that the universe was expanding, Einstein showed that a static universe is unstable according to the equations of General Relativity and postulated a change in the nature of gravity to keep the universe from expanding or contracting. If the universe is not expanding, we would need to find a different explanation for the cosmic microwave background and for the observed percentage of helium in the universe. We would also need to find a new explanation for the redshift and require it to have the following properties: the redshift of a galaxy must be proportional to its distance (Hubble's law) and the same value of $\Delta\lambda/\lambda$ must be obtained for spectral lines in the radio range as in the optical range.

11.   The fact that distant galaxies are moving away from us does not mean that we are the center of the universe. One analogy to the expanding universe is a raisin cake that is rising in the oven. Any raisin in the cake sees the other raisins as moving away from it. Another analogy is a toy balloon that is painted with spots and inflated. In that case, none of the spots is at the center of the expansion, and each spot sees the other spots as receding with velocity proportional to distance.

12.   If you were located near the boundary of our observable universe, you would see galaxies in the direction of the Milky Way as receding from you. The distance between you and the Milky Way is increasing as a result of the expansion of the universe, so each observer sees the other as receding.

13.   The Hubble age is 1/H, where H is the current value of the Hubble parameter. The Hubble age assumes that the expansion of the universe has been constant in time. Because of gravitational attraction between the various masses in the universe, the expansion of the universe has decreased with age, and so the Hubble age is greater than the actual age.

14.   The Big Bang is a uniform expansion. An explosion on Earth is not, since the debris particles all initially travel outwards from the explosion center and subsequently follow parabolic trajectories (except for those particles directed straight up) and come to rest on the ground. The departure angle and the initial speed determine which of the debris particles get the farthest from the center.

For the Big Bang, there is no center and no dependence on angle. For an explosion on Earth and a given value of the departure angle, the debris particles originally moving the fastest get the farthest from the center; only in this rather limited sense is there a "Hubble law" for an explosion on Earth. The debris particles directed straight up correspond to a closed universe, since a closed universe eventually stops expanding and contracts. Debris in other directions corresponds to neither type of universe.

15.   Space-time prior to the primordial nucleus is not defined since the primordial nucleus is the entire universe. Therefore, the primordial nucleus did not expand into anything; it is space-time itself that is expanding.

16.   One can determine that a black hole is present by measuring its gravitational effect on other bodies, as in the following examples.

        a) Some galaxies contain a massive compact object in the center. It is possible to find the mass M of the compact object by using the Doppler shift of the spectral lines to measure the velocities along the line of sight (from Earth) of the material orbiting close to the compact object at a distance r from it. If it is assumed that the measured velocities result from circular motion, the mass of the compact object is given by setting the gravitational acceleration equal to the centripetal acceleration: $GM/r^2 = v^2/r$. (A similar expression applies if the measured velocities represent material streaming towards the compact object.) If the measured radius of the compact object is less than or equal to the Schwarzschild radius, $2GM/c^2$, then the object is a black hole.

        b) Some stars move as if they were orbiting unseen object in a binary system. By measuring the orbital velocity of the star and its distance from the unseen object, one can compute the mass of the unseen object (as above). If the mass of the unseen object in the binary system is substantially greater than that expected for a neutron star, then the unseen object must be a black hole. (If, on the other hand, the mass comes out comparable to the mass of Jupiter, then the unseen object is a planet.)

17.   The cosmic microwave background radiation is blackbody radiation from the very hot, very early stages of the universe. As the universe expanded, this radiation redshifted relative to the observer so the energy of the photons decreased. Since, in blackbody radiation, the temperature T is proportional to $1/\lambda_{peak}$, its temperature decreased as the wavelength λ_{peak} of peak intensity increased.

18.   The term "recombination" implies that originally there was an atomic bond, one supplied energy to break the bond, and then the electron and nucleus came back together to reform the bond. In the case of the universe, when the temperature dropped to about 3000 K, stable atomic bonds were being formed for the first time, so the prefix "re," which means "again," is not appropriate.

19.   At the high temperatures that existed at prior times, photons, electrons, and protons carried sufficient energy so that any atom formed would rapidly be destroyed by collisions with these particles.

20.   The universe is now matter-dominated because there is more energy in the form of matter than in the form of radiation. The wavelength of a photon at the peak intensity of a 2.7 K blackbody is 0.001 m, so it has an energy of 1.3×10^{-3} eV. The rest energy of a proton = 938 MeV, which is a factor of 7.5×10^{11} greater than the energy of the microwave background photon. Dividing this by the 10^9 ratio of the number of photons to the number of baryons, we see that there is more energy in the form of baryons.

21.   If the universe is open, the frequency and the temperature of the microwave background radiation will both decrease toward zero as the age of the universe goes toward infinity. If the universe is closed, it will eventually contract, and during the contraction the background radiation will shift to higher frequencies (blueshift instead of redshift) and its temperature will increase.

22.   If there is enough mass in the universe to give space-time a positive curvature, then the universe is closed and will eventually collapse in on itself. In particular, the universe is closed if the present value of the average mass density exceeds about 10^{-26} kg/m^3.